To: Vernel,

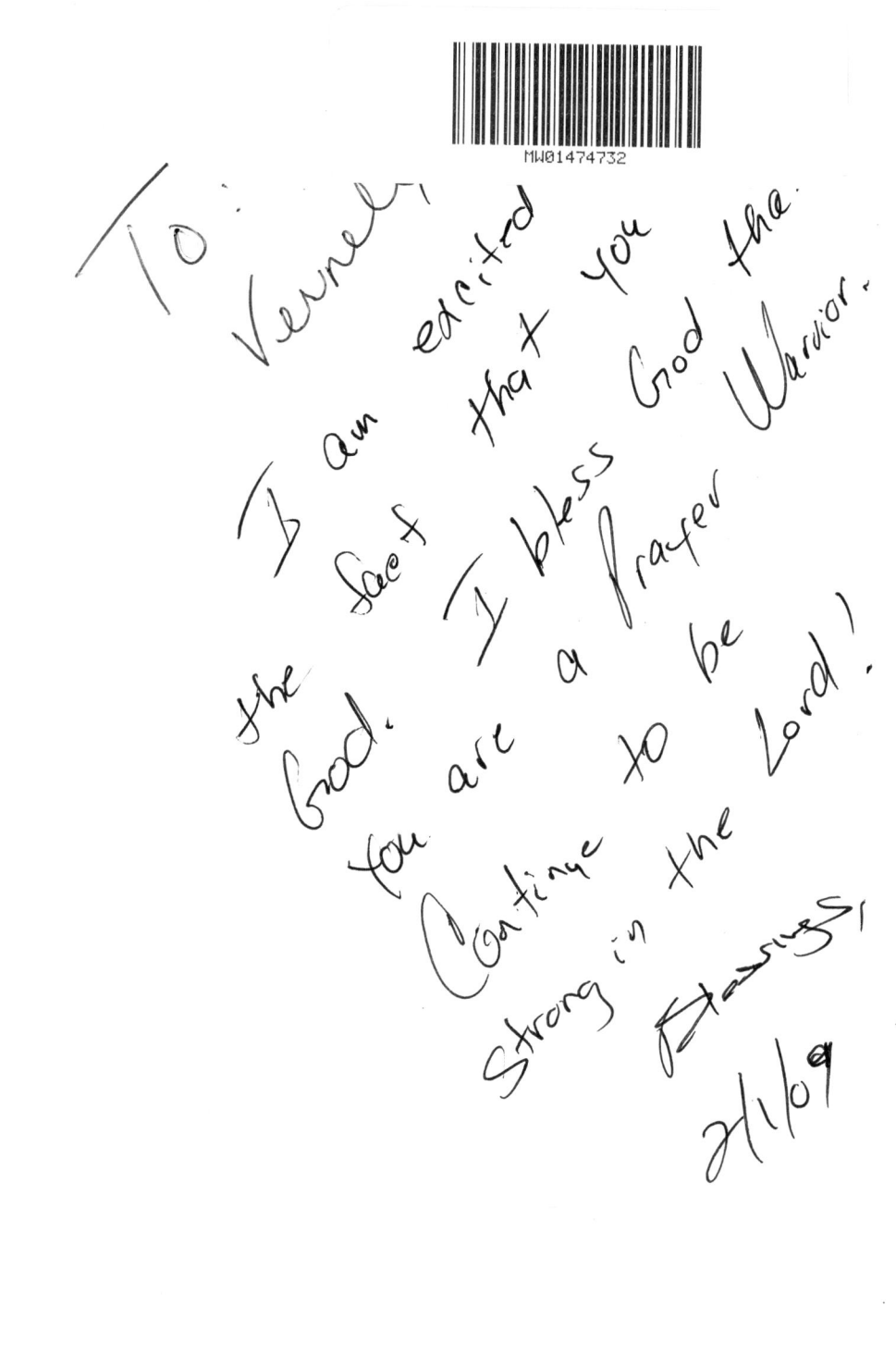

I am excited that you feet the God. I bless God the Warrior. You are a Prayer Warrior. Continue to be strong in the Lord!

Blessings,
2/1/09

Motivation and the Professional African American Woman

by
Dr. Lawanda S. Rutledge

AuthorHouse™
1663 Liberty Drive, Suite 200
Bloomington, IN 47403
www.authorhouse.com
Phone: 1-800-839-8640

This book is a work of non-fiction. Unless otherwise noted, the author and the publisher make no explicit guarantees as to the accuracy of the information contained in this book and in some cases, names of people and places have been altered to protect their privacy.

© 2008 Dr. Lawanda S. Rutledge. All rights reserved.

No part of this book may be reproduced, stored in a retrieval system, or transmitted by any means without the written permission of the author.

First published by AuthorHouse 12/17/2008

ISBN: 978-1-4389-0823-6 (sc)
ISBN: 978-1-4389-0822-9 (hc)

Printed in the United States of America
Bloomington, Indiana

This book is printed on acid-free paper.

DEDICATION

This book is dedicated to the life, legacy, and perseverance of my brother Cornell Mckinney. May Cornell's spirit continue to dwell in our hearts and minds.

ACKNOWLEDGMENTS

I am grateful to God, my Father, for empowering me to exceed expectations and for blessing everything I touch. I salute my best friend and husband Bishop Simon Gordon, for his consistent words of wisdom and knowledge about life and success. I would like to extend my gratitude to the National Black MBA Association Inc. for their cooperation. I also would like to thank the participants for sharing their experiences with the world to make a contribution toward positive change. Finally, I would like to thank my family, especially my mother, Lady Jurdine Rutledge, and father, Pastor Lamont Rutledge, for their prayers and words of encouragement. I look forward to the great success that lies ahead, and I have no room in my heart to accept disappointment. In the words of Bishop Simon Gordon, I have learned in this process to "never conclude a matter, until I have exhausted all of its contradictions." (S. Gordon, personal communication, August 31, 2007).

TABLE OF CONTENTS

DEDICATION v

ACKNOWLEDGMENTS vii

CHAPTER 1: INTRODUCTION TO THE STUDY 1
    Introduction 1
    Statement of the Problem 2
    Purpose of the Research 3
    Research Questions 4
    Significance of the Research 4
    Nature of the Research and Conceptual Framework 5
    Assumptions 6
    Scope and Delimitations 6
    Organization of the Study 7

CHAPTER 2: LITERATURE REVIEW 9
    Introduction 9
    Qualitative Methods 9
    Leadership Theories 11
        Situational Leadership 13
        Positional Leadership 17
        Servant Leader 20
        Transformative Leadership 23
        Trait Leadership 25
        Behavioral Leadership 27
        Summary 30
    Motivation Theories 30
        Motivation 31
        Motivational Factors 32
        Intrinsic/Extrinsic Motivation 33
    Process Theories 34
        Adam's Theory 34
        Vroom's Theory 35
    Needs Theories 40
        Herzberg's Theory 41

        McClelland and Winter's Theory 44
        Maslow's Theory 48
        Alderfer's Theory 50
    Reinforcement Theory 52
    Summary 54

CHAPTER 3: RESEARCH DESIGN METHODOLOGY 55
    Introduction 55
    Research Design 55
        Reliability and Validity 57
        Standards of Quality Verification 57
        Research Questions 58
    Overview of Methodology 59
        Sampling 60
        Participants 60
        Instrument 61
    Data Collection 62
        The Role of the Researcher 62
        Interview 62
        Interview Questions 63
        Demographics 64
        Data Storage 64
    Data Analysis 64
    Ethical Protection 66
    Summary 67

CHAPTER 4: RESULTS AND FINDINGS 69
    Introduction 69
        Research Questions 69
        Methodology 69
        Sample 70
        Table 1. Participants' Demographics 71
    Data Collection 72
    Research Questions Results and Findings 74
        Table 2. Participants' Motivators 75
    Interview Question Results and Findings 76
        Horizonalization 76
        Cluster of Meaning and Thematizing 81

    Composite Textural-structural Description 87
    Triangulation 87
    Summary 89

CHAPTER 5: SUMMARY, CONCLUSION, AND RECOMMENDATIONS 91
    Summary, Conclusion, and Recommendations 91
    Conceptual/Theoretical Framework 92
    Implications for Social Change 92
    Recommendations for Further Study 93
    Conclusion 94

REFERENCES 95

CHAPTER 1: INTRODUCTION TO THE STUDY

Introduction

Organizations are complicated under any circumstances, and no one achieves success without being extraordinary creative, especially in the area of human dynamics. For us there are added layers, but what we had to deal with growing up actually prepared us. We did that every day of our lives, at school, at the store, everywhere outside the home. (David L. Hinds, Managing Director, Deutsche Bank, as cited in Cobbs & Turnock, 2003, p. 1)

The struggle for career achievement, leadership, and a superior life remains a mere aspiration for many African American women in society today. African American women continue to be at the bottom of the leadership ladder. African American women held 1.7 percent of corporate officer positions and were only 1 percent of the top earners of Fortune 500 organizations in 2005 (Nierenberg & Fong, 2006). The quest for leadership positions continues to be a burning desire for many African American women in the United States. An unanswered question is what motivates some African American women to strive and to achieve leadership positions in a world monopolized by male leaders. This book explored what motivated 16 African American female leaders to become leaders in American corporations.

Motivation is the driving force in the choices that humans make to acquire fulfillment and to attain expected results. The Encyclopedia Britannica (n.d.) defined motivation as "forces acting either on or within a person to initiate behavior." This definition insinuates that motivation is purposive behavior in which a mechanism of power or control initiates internally or externally. Motivation is influenced by environmental factors, behavioral factors, and/or internal feelings and emotions. Therefore, motivational factors vary within each individual. Intrinsic motivation is a behavior that is reinforced by learned behavior (Maslow, 1987). This learned behavior is reinforced by pleasure and enjoyment obtained in completing the task successfully or in performing the job. Extrinsic motivation requires a means between the activities, such as a reward or an incentive, to encourage a specific behavior or reaction, as indicated by Gagne (2005).

Maslow (1987) defined motivation as a "parental impulse that guided humans to their destiny, objectives, and purposes in life" (p. 174). Motivation is the force that creates an appetite and a longing to succeed in life. Maslow described motivation as a yearning that must be satisfied through the satisfaction of needs. The satisfaction of needs has many meanings within different ethnic groups. The ethnic group researched in this book was African American women. The identification of the sources of motivation within this group has the power to support a new revolution of leaders within American corporations, according to Daniels (2004).

Statement of the Problem

The research addressed the gap in the lack of understanding regarding what motivates African American women to become corporate leaders. Catalyst, a nonprofit organization that provides research pertaining to women in corporations, published a 2003 report that suggested African American women are under represented in leadership positions within American corporations. There is a lack of understanding about why some African American women are able to obtain leadership positions and others are not. According to that report, African American women make up 13.4 percent of the United States workforce and 5.1 percent of management, professional, and related occupations. In 2001, African American women held 1.6 percent of corporate officer positions within 429 organizations (Catalyst Report). An assumption is made within motivation theories that motivation is standardized behavior without racial or gender barriers. Initiatives to promote minorities, which include every race and gender, with the exception of the Caucasian male, tend to silence the barriers, trials, and discrimination that affect African American women. Despite the increased number of educated African American women in the workplace, the number of African American women in leadership roles continues to remain between 1 percent and 2 percent. In 2001, (National Center for Education Statistics, 2002) African American women earned 73,204 or 5.9 percent of the total bachelors' degrees in the United States.

However, these statistics are not supported by salary variances between gender and race within the United States. For every dollar that a Caucasian man earns, an African American man earns 78 cents, a Caucasian woman earns 74 cents, and an African American woman earns 68 cents (Daniels, 2004). The needs of the African American woman are secondary to the African American man and the Caucasian woman. The African American female voice, silenced during the course of civil rights, has yet to develop a podium from which to speak. The quest to obtain additional information about the motivational experiences of African American women in American corporations was the foundational research question for this phenomenological study.

Purpose of the Research

The purpose of this phenomenological study was to provide academic research on what motivates African American women to be leaders in American corporations. African American women who are motivated to become leaders must first be able to persevere through political challenges. Diversification is becoming crucial to the success of American corporations (Catalyst Report, 2007). Does diversity include African American women, or can a diversified organization meet the needed criteria to be considered diverse with Caucasian female leaders? If the latter is true, exactly where does the African American woman fit into the leadership structure of American corporations? This research is empowered to answer questions such as: what motivates African American women to become leaders in American corporations, and what are barriers that African American women encounter as they strive to achieve leadership roles within American corporations?

This research provides information that will assist African American women in learning how to reach upper leadership levels. American society recognizes that there are racial barriers within American corporations (Catalyst Report, 2003). If specific motivational patterns are identified among African American female leaders, it could lead to more of them being in leadership positions in American corporations.

Research Questions

The following research questions framed this study:
1. What factors do African American women perceive to motivate them to become leaders in American corporations?
2. What are some of the perceived barriers, if any, for African American women as they pursue leadership roles?

Significance of the Research

The significance of this study was the documentation of academic research to galvanize awareness and understanding of motivation factors among African American women. With an enhanced understanding of motivation among African American women, corporations will be able to effectively target the needs of African American women to identify more leaders. Leaders, according to Bass and Stogdill (1990), are agents of change. Leaders, according to Bennis (2000), are people who change the substance of their practices as well as their discipline. This means that leaders have the ability to diversify their techniques and their style to meet the needs of the environment. Bass and Stogdill defined leadership as "an interaction between two or more members of a group that involves a structuring or restructuring of the situation and the perception and expectations of the members" (p. 19).

An effective leader is the catalyst for a metamorphosis of mindset, thought process, and lifestyle among their followers. A leader should have the ability to challenge the follower's intellect to strive to be more, to do more, and to achieve within life. Limits of success should not be stifled by attitudes, behaviors, or personalities when the appropriate leader is leading the appropriate group of followers with the appropriate leadership style, which should be individualized to meet the needs and the expectations of the followers (Bass and Stogdill, 1990). This research challenges the status quo concept and theories of practice among leaders in American corporations to focus on the African American woman and the barriers within the organization.

A deeper understanding of barriers that hinder African American women from becoming leaders should open new avenues of opportunity in the corporate community for more African American women to lead. The completion of this research provides encouragement for future generations of African American women to strive and to acquire leadership opportunities in American corporations.

Nature of the Research and Conceptual Framework

This research was a qualitative research study that utilized a phenomenological research method. The aim was to determine what motivated 16 African American women to become leaders within American corporations. The researcher derived general and universal meanings of motivation and barriers from data collected during telephone interviews with African American women, currently in leadership positions, and linked this data to existing motivation theories in the literature. Open-ended questions were asked to obtain core life experiences through first-person accounts. Common bonds and patterns were identified and conceptualized into a narrative description of the experiences shared among the participants via a procedure called meaning structuring through narratives (Kvale, 1996). The motivational theories of Maslow (1987), McClelland and Winter (1969), Herzberg (1997), Adams (1963), Vroom (1995), and Alderfer (Miner, 2002) were explored to obtain a better understanding of human motivation. The leadership theories of Greenleaf (2002), Blake and Mouton (1985), Blanchard, D. Zigarmi, and K. Zigarmi (1985), Maxwell (1993), Bass and Stogdill (1990), and Burns (1978) were examined to establish a baseline of possible leadership styles.

Assumptions

This research assumed the following:
1. African American women have unique barriers that hinder their ability to obtain leadership roles in American corporations.
2. African American women are under-represented in American corporations.
3. African American women's drive to lead in American corporation is related to personal motivation.
4. Motivation is correlated with success among African American women.
5. It is perceived that African American women leaders are an endangered species without a voice within American corporations.
6. The needs of African American women are perceived to be secondary to those of the African American man and the Caucasian woman.

Scope and Delimitations

The scope of this study was limited due to the miniscule percentage of African American women in leadership roles in American corporations. The researcher interviewed a sample of 16 African American women to obtain life experiences related to motivation, barriers, and opportunities for leadership roles in American corporations. This study also was limited to the experiences and viewpoints of African American women who have obtained a leadership position in an American corporation. The researcher did not conduct interviews with African American women who currently are pursuing a leadership opportunity within an American corporation. Though referenced, the researcher did not address the viewpoints of African American men in this research. In addition, viewpoints of other ethnic groups were not obtained for this research. This study was expanded to include African Americans throughout the United States.

Organization of the Study

Chapter 1 provided an introduction to the research, as well as an overview of motivation and leadership. The problem statement, purpose of the study, limitations, and research concept also are located in Chapter 1. Chapter 2 includes the literature review, which is a framework of past research explored on the targeted participants, the phenomena, and relevant material. Chapter 3 incorporates the research design, methodology, data collections, and data analysis of the research. Chapter 4 presents the findings and results. Chapter 5 provides a summary, conclusion, and recommendations, and implication for social change.

CHAPTER 2: LITERATURE REVIEW

Introduction

Chapter 2 provides a literature review related to the problem statement, including an integrative review and a methodological review. The integrative review represented the state of the knowledge relevant to motivation and leadership. Several motivational and leadership theories were explored to complete the literature review.

Qualitative Methods

Qualitative research was employed to answer questions pertaining to motivation, to explore the motivation of African American women leaders, and to present detailed views of the experiences of African American women in leadership roles. Qualitative research design can be subdivided into five studies: biography, ethnography, grounded theory, case study, and phenomenology. Each research method has a distinguished approach and design representing a continuum of research methodology. The ethnography is the foundation of the continuum of research. The objective of ethnography is to explore cultures, settings, social groups, and geographies to learn the patterns, behaviors, and customs of particular groups, with its success being dependent on extensive fieldwork. The ethnography research consists of explorations, planning, and intensive preparation, which includes obtaining permission for observation and participation, or a plan development for site visits (Moustakas, 1994). Ethnography is challenging to use because of the extensive time to collect data, the possibility that the researcher will become too involved in the research and will be unable to complete the study, and the need for the researcher to have a foundation in cultural anthropology and to understand the cultural system being studied, according to Creswell (1998).

The grounded theory research that emphasizes analysis and discovery to explain an individual or a group reaction to a phenomenon is at the opposite end of the research continuum. The data collection method is primary interviews with multiple field visits to observe behaviors. According to Creswell (1998), "The centerpiece of grounded theory research is the development or generation of a theory closely related to the context of the phenomenon being studied" (p. 56). Some challenges of grounded theory include: (a) allocation of time to analyze and process theoretical ideas and notions, (b) organization and specific planning of steps to structure data analysis, (c) determination of broad and detailed categorizing, and (d) recognition of a theory as the outcome of research.

The heart of the continuum of qualitative research methodology is the case study Creswell postulated (1998). The case study is "an exploration of a bounded system or a case over time through detailed, in-depth data collection involving multiple sources of information rich in context" (Creswell, p.61). The data collection method of case studies includes documents, archival records, interviews, observations, and physical artifacts. Some challenges of case studies include: (a) identification of the specific case, (b) identification of multiple or single case studies, (c) identification of a purposeful sampling strategy, (d) obtaining adequate information, and (e) identification of the boundaries of the case study.

Phenomenon, the root word of phenomenology, means to "bring to light, to place in brightness, to show itself in itself, the totality of what lies before us in the light of the day" (Moustakas, 1994, p. 28). Phenomenology describes the life experiences of individuals based upon a phenomenon. Challenges of the phenomenology method are: (a) obtaining foundational information of the philosophical perceptions of the concept, (b) sampling participants that experienced the phenomenon, (c) clustering and bracketing data appropriately, and (d) identifying bias within the study, as indicated by Creswell (1998).

Understanding the philosophical perception of the concepts means that the researcher must analyze personal perceptions of the phenomenon to operate as a voice of the participants, according to Creswell (1998). This statement means that the researcher designed questions based upon perceived ideas of motivation within the African American community. Next, the researcher collected a sample of participants that experienced the phenomenon of leadership. For the purpose of this study, the sample was drawn from African American women in leadership positions within an American corporation. An example of clustering is collecting the results from the transcribed interviewers and grouping the statements into themes by removing repetitive statements. This process becomes a challenge because the researcher must maintain the integrity of each participant's statement to ensure an understanding of the shared experiences. The researcher also needs to monitor or pay attention to potential bias. For the purpose of this research paper, one potential source of bias was the cultural background of the researcher. Although this factor was believed to aid in understanding the experiences of participants, the researcher needed to be able to express the principal meaning of the participants' experiences as it relates to motivation.

Leadership Theories

The definition of leadership is as diverse as the styles and theories of leadership. To have one basic definition of leadership would limit the evolution, understanding, and exploration of the various entities within the word leadership, and the role of leadership within the ancient and present society. Greenleaf (2002), Maxwell (1993), and Burns (2003) have based the definition of leadership with the foundation of their beliefs of leadership as well as their experience of leaders during their lifespan

Burns (2003) defined leadership as "the reciprocal process of mobilizing, by persons with certain motives and values, various economic, political, and other resources, in a context of competition and conflict, in order to realize goals independently or mutually held by both leaders and followers" (p. 425). Leadership, in Burns's language, equates to power, motivation, ethics, challenges, and tools within the control and power of the leader to disseminate to the followers in a useful manner. Although the leader maintains and holds the power within the group, the ability to control does not necessarily make a person a leader. The ability to control and to maintain power is only a minute aspect of the prominent qualities of a leader. Burns explained that a leader has purposeful power that is not only collective but also relational and relevant to the followers. This purposeful power aids in establishing and achieving objectives within the organization. For the purpose of this study, the working definition of leadership was the definition provided by Burns.

Leadership that is open to anyone within an institution who has value, patience, and competence is the mindset of Greenleaf's (2002) servant leader. Greenleaf defined a leader as one who goes first and who shows the way. A leader provides directions, guidance, and empowerment to the followers, with great emphasis on being a servant first. This form of leadership skill is observed more within the academic and religious world and less likely in the business industry, with the exception of Southwest Airlines. Southwest Airlines incorporated the servant leadership style in the day-to-day operations of its organization. A leader is a servant to the followers serving in skill, understanding, and spirit (Greenleaf). The servant leader provides the follower with everything needed to be successful.

Maxwell (2000) believed that true leadership is based on influence. The first task of leadership, according to Maxwell, is the ability to influence others to follow, since a leader cannot lead without followers. Maxwell suggested that everyone has the capability to influence someone; the question is whether the level of influence is positive or negative. Maxwell believed that leaders have the ability to adapt the skill to influence followers to achieve consistently positive things, to strive to go positive places, and to strive to be positive people.

The development of positive people is connected to the leadership style of the leader. Greenleaf (2002) and Maxwell (1993) asserted that followers are only as great as their leader. For this reason, Blanchard et al., (1985) believed that true leaders have the ability to adapt to the style that is most conducive to the developmental growth of followers. As employees are hired with a diversified array of skill sets, Blanchard et al., stated that the leaders should learn to coach to strengths and weakness in order to better develop the follower and to expand growth potential. A true leader is able to individualize his or her leadership style to meet the needs of the team and to aid in moving the team forward successfully.

Situational Leadership

Blanchard's et al. (1985) situational leadership theory is utilized in corporations throughout the United States. The authors proposed that the essence of knowledge is having it and using it. This means that sharing what you know is just as important as knowing what you know. The situational leader, according to Blanchard et al., suggested that managers should work for their people. Successful leaders spend time with employees to identify what specific skills are needed to be successful on the job as well as for career development. The leader and employee discuss realistic and achievable goals that will guarantee success for both the company and the employee. To set unrealistic goals will only produce failure for both the leader and the employee and will serve as a demotivator. Blanchard et al., noted that another key factor when identifying goals and understanding the needs of the employees is to develop "different strokes for different folks" (p. 19). The situational leaders recognize that while micromanaging works for some employees, others enjoy working independently on tasks to stretch their level of creativity and ability to discover solutions.

American educator Juliette Derricotte is an example of a situational leader, one who worked for people across international cultures and races and tailored her leadership style to meet the needs of her followers. As a member of the National Student Council of the YWCA, Derriocotte is credited with creating an interracial fellowship within the council (Franklin & Meier, 1982). Derriocotte welcomed diversity challenges and problems and spent her abbreviated life promoting justice and equality for all people, her global community.

Blanchard et al. (1985) stated that a problem only occurs when there is a variance between what is happening and what is desired. This statement usually causes the employee to think deeply to identify exactly what the desired outcome should resemble. This thought process aids in discovering several solutions that are open enough for the leader and the employee to reach a compromise as it relates to solutions. The next phase is implementation. During this phase, the situational leader will lead by skill set. If the employee is tenured and experienced enough to develop an implementation plan independent of the leader, the leader encourages the employee to do so with his or her support, if needed. If the employee is new to the task or is not comfortable enough, the leader will provide more hands-on help with the implementation by providing guidelines, directives, and closely monitored support. When an employee is in the middle stage of development, a leader has the task of finding the employee's comfort level with implementation and coaching by using direct, yet passive leadership skills to encourage employee independence. One of the major focal points of the situational leader is to balance the level of encouragement provided to employees to manage themselves based upon the employee's skills set and level of comfort with the leader.

One of the major roles of the situational leader is to develop a leadership style that is conducive to the employee's environment and style of learning. Directing, coaching, supporting, and delegating are the four leadership styles of a situational leader. The situational leadership theory has a foundation that is based upon four leadership styles. Although Blanchard's et al. (1985) leadership style is different from other leadership styles, the situational leadership theory encompasses a variety of combinations of each style to individualize the leadership skills of the leader. This means that each employee is led differently based on skill set, competency, and career development. Blanchard et al. noted that the leader has the liberty to simultaneously lead by directing and coaching some employees, and by supporting and coaching other employees.

When using a direct leadership style (Style I), the leader provides clear and concise direction while closely monitoring tasks and assignments. With this style, the level of support is minimal. The leader focuses on providing clear expectations while also giving directives about how specific tasks should be completed (Blanchard et al., 1985). When a problem arises, the leader makes the decision on the resolution and the employee carries out the plan. This is observed in the pharmaceutical sales industry when sales performance is low. Directives are given to sales representatives to increase call frequency in order to boost sales. The sales representative has little input in providing directives, yet is very active in carrying out the directive in efforts to solve the problem of poor sales performance. The manager usually coaches the sales representative to provide clear sales expectations.

Style II of situational leadership is coaching. Many leaders consider themselves coaches. Motivational speakers advertise themselves as life coaches. Blanchard et al. (1985) described the coaching leadership style as directing and closely monitoring task accomplishments, as well as explaining decisions, requesting input, and supporting progress. Coaching is leading through open communication by using dialogue. Burns (2003), like Blanchard et al., believed that the role of the leader is to assist in the development of the followers.

Although the manager is clearly the leader, the input of the employee is valuable and, therefore, is encouraged by the manager. The coaching style connects both directing and supporting leadership styles to produce more of a team environment (Blanchard et al., 1985). Coaching is typically used when the employee has taken on a task that appears to be overwhelming; the manager is in place to provide consistent encouragement and support. Supporting the employee's good ideas, thoughts, and concepts while developing the employee's ability to evaluate his or her own work reinforces the worker's motivation by allow the employee to have a more active role.

Supporting is Blanchard's et al. (1985) third style of situational leadership (Style III). Supporting includes sharing the decision making process with employees as well as facilitating and supporting the efforts of employees. Experienced employees characteristically prefer the supporting style because they prefer to be managed with a more participative management style. Using the supporting style allows the employee to exercise areas of strength and yet still obtain support in areas of weakness. In the pharmaceutical sales industry, managers who have executive representatives on their team use this style. Executive representatives are normally charged with more difficult tasks, such as providing inservices about products to the vice presidents of the organization. The manager provides support while coaching to the executive representatives' areas of strengths. When areas of insecurity or hesitation occur, the manager provides support to assist in completing the task successfully. Usually, managers have insight into which executive representatives are able to complete the task before delegating the task to the executive representative.

The final type of the four leadership styles is delegating, which is the act of turning over responsibility and problem solving to the employee. In Style IV, the employee has the task of making the decision as well as implementing the needed steps to solve the problem (Blanchard et al., 1985). Maxwell's (1993) positional leadership theory focuses more on developing the employee before assigning the task. Blanchard et al. believed that "self-reliant achievers" are the best employees to lead by delegation because they are knowledgeable, proficient, and committed (p. 42). Self-reliant achievers are characterized as employees that need little support, minimal coaching, clear direction, and consistent feedback. The consistent feedback is very important when using the delegating style because employees are able to gauge their progress throughout the problem solving stages. The secret to being a great situational leader is awareness and development of what style works best with each employee (Blanchard et al.).

Blanchard et al. (1985), unlike Bass and Stogdill (1990), stated, "The skill of diagnosing a situation before you act is the key to being a situational leader" (p. 43). As the leader of a group, some of the major objectives are: to see the situation differently from employees, to know the competency level of each employee, and to recognize which leadership style or combination of styles works best with each employee. A situational leader takes time to engage employees to develop a better understanding of where the employee is and at what level of function this employee operates best. The situational leader considers past working experience, level of knowledge, comfort, and level of security before implementing a specific leadership style. Similar to Maxwell (1993), Blanchard et al. believed that influence is fundamental to leadership; however, he did not believe that leadership is influence.

Positional Leadership

Maxwell (1993) took leadership to another dimension by defining leadership as influence. Leaders have the ability to obtain and to maintain followers through influence. If a person is unable to obtain followers, this person is not a leader. Positional leadership consists of five levels of leadership, and many leaders are only successful in effectively obtaining four. Position, permission, production, people development, and personhood are the five areas of influence or leadership (Maxwell). Wells is an example of a positional leader within the African American community. Recognized as an outspoken propagandist with influence, Ms. Wells was a feminist and an anti-lynching spokesperson with a host a followers (Franklin & Meier, 1982).

Position is the entry level of leadership that is obtained by having a title. When a former employee is promoted to a leadership role, he or she is at the position level of leadership. The following characteristics apply to a positional leader: security is not based on talent, but on title; position is gained by appointment; influence is limited to stated authority; and the leader is unable to lead volunteers, white-collar workers, and younger people. During the position level, the leader that operates with little confidence will have employees with little confidence. No matter in what level a leader is currently functioning, Maxwell (1993) believed that the employees have the same spirit and outlook of the leader. When a leader is positive, employees are positive. The key to being a successful positional leader is to know how to make a timely transition through the various levels. If the "position level is the door, then the permission level is the foundation" (Maxwell, p. 8). The best positional leader recognizes that the position level is temporary and transitions immediately into the permission level.

During the permission level, the leader's objective is to build relationships with employees to obtain indirectly the permission he or she needs to influence employees. The permission level incorporates the core of the leader. Meaningful relationships, interrelationships, and people development become essential at the permission level. Employees are concerned about the leader's level of commitment to them, as well as how much the leader cares. Permission is considered the foundation because leadership is built on relationships, trust, security, and level of comfort (Maxwell, 1993). Employees must have a sense of connection or belonging to follow by influence.

Burns (1978) believed that the establishment of relationship with followers is vital to the success of the leader. Leaders are not able to have a productive tea unless the tea has established some form of relationship that enables them to enjoy one another. The leader obtains permission to lead by developing relationships with the team while encouraging team building. Blanchard et al.,1985 theory differs from Maxwell's (1993) during this phase, due to the lack of emphasis on teambuilding. In Blanchard et al., the focus is primarily on the relationship of the leader and the employee on an individual level. Maxwell highlighted the development of relationships between the leader and the follower, whereas Blanchard and Johnson (2003) highlighted the development of the employee.

According to Maxwell (2000), once the employees and leader feel comfortable enough to come together frequently, the next level is to come together to increase productivity. The third level is production, which is where sales increase, morale increases, production increases, and turnover decreases. Problem solving becomes a daily task because the level of comfort among employees and leadership has increased based upon well-established relationships. It is at this stage the team becomes more "relationship-oriented" and less task-oriented (Maxwell, 1993, p. 9). Although Maxwell, unlike Blanchard et al. (1985), does not include coaching as one of his levels, the concept of coaching is a part of the positional leadership theory. Success is likely because the employees and the leader are together on a team where the leader is the coach. Usually, successful teams have several successful members that consistently exceed expectations.

The fourth level of leadership is people development, which is done through coaching. Maxwell (2000) suggested that leaders are great because of their ability to empower others. According to Maxwell, great leaders have learned to develop others, which means that the employees are groomed to become better leaders than the one they are succeeding.

Maxwell (1993) said little about level five due to his belief that many leaders never reach this level. Personhood, or level five, is when the leader's influence causes employees to follow because of "who the leader is and what the leader represents" (p. 13). This is referent power, or charisma in the power/influence literature. Only a small percentage of leaders reach this level due to their lack of experience and confidence in themselves and their leadership skills. An example of a leader that reached stage five is Dr. Martin Luther King, Jr. According to Maxwell, when a leader's legacy outlives him by decades, he has achieved the personhood level.

Beyond the five levels of positional leadership, Maxwell (2000) added some key takeaways that will assist in preventing escalated areas of concern within an organization. They include integrity, positive change, problem solving, attitude, people, vision, self-discipline, and staff development. Maxwell believed integrity to be the most important ingredient of leadership. In order to be acknowledged as a leader of integrity, a leader must ensure that what is said lines up with what is done. Employees pay more attention to actions than to words. A leader must learn to do what has been said and to say what will be done. Empty promises may cause confusion and areas of distrust between the leader and the team.

Another aspect of leadership that connects Maxwell (2000) and Blanchard et al. (1985) is the idea that leaders are the first change agents. The leader must positively portray any form of change. When a leader is confident, the followers are confident (Maxwell). Having a positive attitude will encourage positive employees as well as a positive working environment. Another key concept is the importance of a vision, which is the organization's direction and foresight. Greenleaf (2002), borrowing from Maxwell's theory (1993, p.139), believed that foresight is the "lead" that the leader has. Maxwell believed that a leader with a vision does much, talks little, and is stimulated by self-convictions. The leader must see beyond the vision of the followers to observe the reality of the past and to evaluate the status of the present to predict the direction of the future.

Servant Leader

Greenleaf's (2002) servant leadership theory is similar to Maxwell's (1993) positional leadership theory due to the religious foundation of godly principles. However, Greenleaf focused on serving first and leading second, whereas Maxwell's (1993) approach is the opposite. Maxwell (1993) believed the foundation of leadership is influence. A servant leader, according to Greenleaf, leads through serving his followers.

Mary McLeod Bethune, an African American educator, political advisor, and civil rights leader lived the life of a servant leader. As the architect of Florida's Bethune Cookman College, Bethune ensured that African American children had a place to advance their educations. As the founder and president of the National Council of Negro Women, she ensured that African Americans had a voice in the federal bureaucracy during the Franklin D. Roosevelt administration (Franklin & Meier, 1982) because she had established trust within the African American community.

To be followed, trust must be elicited (Greenleaf, 2002). Although Maxwell (1993) placed great emphasis on trust, Greenleaf suggested that a leader could not function without trust, such that the emphasis on influence without trust is minute. In order to be an effective servant leader, attributes of both traits must be obviously manifested. Although Greenleaf did not include stages, levels, or phases, he did point out several talents that are very important to the servant leader. Greenleaf asserted that the ability to listen and to understand is the foundation to the servant leader. Leading as a servant means that the leader must take the time to identify and to understand the needs of the followers. Development of understanding comes through observing, listening, and interacting with the followers. Many leaders take on a role and begin to give direction, tentative solutions, and assignments without initially understanding the problems, areas of concern, past successes, and past failure. According to Greenleaf, a servant leader has the ability to not only to hear followers, but also listen to followers and learn to speak their language.

Another skill of a servant leader is the ability to use language and imagination to proactively lead the followers into unfound areas of achievement (Greenleaf, 2002). As the leader listens to the followers, it is important that the leader have the skills to understand the language of the followers well enough to understand both what is said aloud and what remains unspoken. Greenleaf suggested that the ability to use experiences and imagination to translate the language of employees requires great people skills and the ability to accept people for who they are in various settings.

Acceptance and empathy is Greenleaf's (2002) third talent of the servant leader. The servant leader has learned to accept people and to reject inappropriate characteristics, traits, and behaviors. As the servant leader is accepting and empathic, the challenge is to continue to understand and to provide emotion, making sure expectations are clear and consistent. Blanchard and Johnson's (1985) situational leader theory is very similar to the servant leadership theory in the area of expectations, as he noted that expectations should be clear.

According to Greenleaf (2002), the servant leader should know the unknowable. Burns's (1978) consciousness of the leader is another way of maintaining an awareness of one's surroundings. This means that the servant leader must be in tune with himself or herself enough to feel comfortable with following inner assumptions. Greenleaf postulated that the servant leader who moves by intuition has established a foundation of trust that may enhance foresight.

Maxwell (1993) and Greenleaf (2002) agreed that a leader should have foresight, recognizing that a vision provides direction and guidance to the future and that the presence of foresight provides the light leading to the future. Greenleaf defined foresight as, "regarding the events of the instant moment and constantly comparing them with a series of projections made in the past and at the same time projecting future events" (p. 39). In order to function fully as a servant leader, the leader must understand the history of the organization. This understanding may be accomplished by listening to the follower's problems, by generating solutions and having the experience to recognize what will work, and by knowing what will not work for the organization via awareness and perception.

The sixth talent of the servant leader, according to Greenleaf (2002), is awareness and perception. The servant leader has the ability to obtain awareness while allowing his or her perception to influence decisions or level of confidence. During this stage of leadership, the servant leader must learn to clarify and reevaluate before making hasty decisions. The servant leader also must trust and carry out decisions while recognizing mistakes and flaws. One of the key concepts in awareness and perceptions is that right may not always be fair, and fair may not always be right. This is why the integrity of the servant leader is very important. As Maxwell

(1993) stated, the followers must learn and understand the heart of the leader.

The servant leader also has the talent of persuasion. Maxwell (1993) described that this talent has influence. Although Greenleaf (2002) did not believe that leadership is influence alone, he recognized that the servant leader must be able to persuade followers. The goal of the servant leader is to win the loyalty and respect of the followers through persuasion. Loyalty through persuasion does not have to be by the masses. Greenleaf believed that persuasion occurs one follower at a time.

Transformative Leadership

Burns's (1978) described the transforming leader as one who "recognizes and exploits an existing need or demand of a potential follower" (p. 4). The transforming leader seeks to identify motivators, needs, and aspirations of followers. This leader strives to make the follower a leader. Burns's (1978) theory resembles Maxwell's (1993) theory of mentoring a successor. Ella Jo Baker, the National Association for the Advancement of Colored People (NAACP) Field Secretary, was one of the first female transformational leaders within the African American community (Parker, 2005). The focal point of Baker's transforming leadership style was to organize African Americans to define their own problems, formulate their own questions, and develop their own solutions (Parker). According to Parker, this principle encouraged African American leaders to become moral agents.

Burns (1978) described transforming leadership at a greater level by renaming transforming leadership moral leadership. This level of moral leadership is based on the leader's ability to meet the needs of the followers: moral leadership is similar to servant leadership in that the objective is to serve the followers by identifying their wants, needs, aspirations, and values. The second step after identifying these areas is to act upon them by providing consistent implementation guides that are based upon the level of integrity of the leader. When comparing Maxwell's (1993) and Greenleaf's (2002) theories, both believed that the leader must ensure that the language provided is consistent with the action given, and both have a spiritual base of assumptions.

Transforming leadership, according to Burns (1978), concerns the relationship between the leader and the follower. The concept of transforming leadership is established upon power and values, conflict and consciousness, and elevating power. Burns marked a clear stance on the expectation of political leaders by stating that they must be willing to make enemies. Recognizing that leadership can include having the power of influence without values, the transformative leader must balance the two. It is clear and concise that the transforming leader must make his or her stance very clear, while recognizing that some people might oppose established beliefs. For the opposing viewer, such as Greenleaf (2002) the intelligent transforming leader must carefully select followers that are committed not only to the leader's beliefs but also to the leader through relationships. This form of leadership is evident in the political arena, where the leader's views may change; however, followers seldom change political parties.

Burns (1978) believed that competition and conflict are a part of leadership and that leaders should make conscious choices to manage conflict effectively. Transforming leadership is quite different from situational as well as positional leadership in that it appears almost to welcome defiance in an effort to motivate followers. True followers of transforming leadership engage the motives, values, and goals of their leaders. What this means is the transforming leader has taken the time to learn not only about the follower but also about the family, friends, and colleagues of the follower to obtain a more comprehensive examination of their needs, desires, and wants (Burns). Many transforming leaders recognize that conflict is a part of relationship, so instead of avoiding conflict, the transforming leader embraces conflict consciously (Burns). Burns stated that true consciousness is accomplished through "unremitting conflict" (p. 40). If leadership is influence, according to Maxwell (1993), the transforming leader must lead to influence the intensity of conflict to obtain continuous success.

The final aspect of leadership, according to Burns (1978), is the elevating power of leadership. The transforming leader, at this stage, has the ability to operate at levels greater than followers and to display conflict and strain within a follower's value structure. This means that the transforming leader believes that ability to debate issues is helpful for the development of the employee. It is at this stage that the leader takes the form of a teacher by revealing areas of contradictions or discrepancies between values and behavior. The leader can encourage reevaluations of aspirations and gratifications to motivate the follower to reach higher dimensions of obtaining objectives through consistent behaviors.

Trait Leadership

Bass and Stogdill (1990) conducted a study measuring the influence of traits to the relationship of leadership potential and success based on the results of 163 studies. The areas of interest included: leadership and activity level; task competence and leadership; interpersonal competence and leadership; authoritarianism, power orientation, machiavellians, and leadership; values, needs, and well-being of leaders; and status, esteem, and leadership. The results indicated that each of the above areas directly affected the success and potential of success of leaders. Bass and Stogdill's based their theory upon the leader's ability to demonstrate a trait, which in turn can predict their level of success as it relates to leadership.

Bass and Stogdill's (1990) study of leader activity levels indicated that leaders needed to be more active and to have a high level of spontaneity. The results indicated that people are influenced by active, energetic, assertive people. Similar to many of the theorists explored in this research, such as Burns (2003), Maxwell (1993), and Blanchard and Johnson (2003), Bass and Stogdill believed that leaders influenced followers. High energy, participative leaders tend to encourage followers to be energetic and active within the organization. The key to this trait of leadership is to focus on leading by example. Therefore, leaders that are task driven will have followers that are task driven.

Another trait identified by Bass and Stogdill (1990) is task competence. Many of the studies showed a correlation between intelligence and leadership indicating that many leaders tended to be more intelligent than followers. The authors associated intelligence with task competence, indicating that intelligent leaders are more apt to be competent in completing tasks successfully. This is evident within the academic arena when instructors are able to complete word problems that students have yet to understand. Another important trait in this category is the ability to use intuition as a mechanism to make decisions. Bass and Stogdill, like Burns (1978), stressed the importance of intuition as the foundation of developing leadership skills for the successful leader.

Burns believed that the ability to communicate with others is one of the growing traits of successful leadership (2003), with leaders being unable to lead if they are unable to influence followers. The ability to influence occurs via relationships. Bass and Stogdill (1990), in comparison to Burns (1978), placed greater emphasis on the insight and empathy of followers. Leaders must seek to understand before they are able to place judgment on a particular behavior or trait. Listening is an important part of understanding followers and their constantly changing behavior. When leaders learn to build relationships, their influence will go far beyond the title of leader of a particular group or area.

The next trait identified by Bass and Stogdill (1990) is the authority, power, and Machiavellianism of the leader. Machiavelli, according to Bass and Stogdill, "was an early amoral behaviorist who argued for studying what we do, rather than what we ought to do" (p. 134). Machiavellianism is the ability to lead with power without any implication of guilt or disgrace. The results of the study indicated that in certain settings, such as the classroom or in military environments, authoritative leadership traits are well accepted and expected. However, the diverse leader recognizes when to use power and authority and when not to use power and authority to motivate employees, Bass and Stogdill described this process as Machiavellianism. Leaders who are motivated by power can be effective leaders if they also focus on being task oriented, according to Bass and Stogdill.

Bass and Stogdill (1990) noted that many organizations employ leaders due to their commitment to the values, view, and mission of the organization. Once hired, it is vital that the leader's values parallel the leader's actions. Although compensation is a strong motivator of employees as well as leaders, its impact does not predict a leader's ability to lead. Bass and Stogdill stated, "projected needs for achievement and task orientation contribute positively to the emergence of leaders" (p.165), which means that a leader must understand his or her needs, values, and aspirations to lead a team into the direction that is vital to success.

The final trait of status, according to Bass and Stogdill (1990), aids in the leader's level of influence because followers tend to pay closer attention to leaders with high status. Employees who are striving to obtain higher positions tend to value leaders with higher positions within an organization. Bass and Stogdill believe that the value and worth of a leader increases as he or she moves to higher echelons (p. 170). As leaders excel within an organization, responsibility and authority increase, providing an increase in status and power. With the increase of power and status, the leader usually excels in esteem from employees. Although the development of certain traits is a useful tool in measuring the successful of a leader, according to Bass & Stogdill, the behavior of the leader is essential to the leader's ability to maintain a leadership role.

Behavioral Leadership

The Managerial Grid III, established by Blake and Mouton (1985), provided a visual grid of leadership by plotting a leader's variance between concern for production and concern for people on the x and y axes. Similar to Burns (2003), Blanchard et al. (1985), and Maxwell (1993), Blake and Mouton suggested that a leader's ability to lead is based upon organizational skills, values, personal history, and chance. Five possible leadership styles are plotted on the chart based upon the leader's motives, ability to manage conflict, behavior skills, and management practices, according to Blake and Mouton.

The first leadership style, according to Blake and Mouton (1985), is the 9, 1 leadership style. This leadership style is plotted at the lower right corner of the grid. The 9 indicates a high concern for production, whereas the 1 indicates a low concern for people. The 9, 1 leader is authoritative and enjoys driving others to produce. This leader takes pleasure in investigating beliefs, facts, and positions to ensure continuous control over employees. Little to no attention is paid to the emotions, status, or growth of employees. The 9, 1 leader can be successful; however, it usually is at the cost of the employees or other colleagues. Many leaders that function by using the 9, 1 leadership style could benefit from adapting some of Greenleaf's (2002) servant leadership traits.

The total opposite of the 9, 1 leadership style is the 1, 9 leadership style. The top left corner of the grid houses the 1, 9 leader. This leader has low concern for production and high concern for people. Some of the key motivators for the 1, 9 leader are developing people, motivating people, helping people, and building relationships with people. This leader avoids conflict whenever possible in order to ensure strong relationships. Employees tend to love working for the 1, 9 leader; however, success and good results happen by chance (Blake & Mouton, 1985). The 1, 9 leaders would benefit from Blanchard's et al. (1985) situational leadership style by providing a consistent balance between developing people and producing results.

The balance between concern for people and concern for production is noted in Blake and Mouton's (1985) 5, 5 leadership style. This leader, found in the center of the grid, is noted as the middle leader. The 5, 5 leader strives to motivate employees to solve problems, to handle conflict by finding reasonable mediums , and to provide consistent feedback while maintaining consistent results. The 5, 5 leader is most similar to Blanchard's et al. (1985) situational leadership style, in that Blake and Mouton (1985) focus on balance and leading according to specific situations. The 5, 5 leader helps employees through consistent feedback and development and helps the organization by developing employees that produce consistent results.

The balance between concern for people and concern for production is a challenging balance to obtain. The 1, 1 leader, according to Blake and Mouton (1985), really struggles in this area. Leaders that have low concern for people and low concern for production are found in the lower left corner of the grid. The 1, 1 leader strives to do just enough – say just enough, perform just enough, and support just enough – to maintain his or her position. Employees are not a concern, as evidenced by little to no feedback. When conflict arises, this leader maintains a neutral opinion and allows others to make concrete decisions. The 1, 1 leader could benefit from reviewing Bass and Stogdill's (1990) trait leadership theory to develop a better understanding of specific traits of successful and long-lasting leaders.

Blake and Mouton's (1985) final leadership style is the 9, 9 leader, plotted in the upper right corner of the grid. The 9, 9 leader has a high concern for people and a high concern for production. This leadership style provides a great correlation between Blanchard's et al. (1985) situational leadership theory, Bass and Stogdill's (1990) trait theory, and Maxwell's (1993) positional leader theory. People development, a task driven orientation, listening skills, conflict resolution skills, sound decision making skills, and motivation are some of the essential traits of the 9, 9 leader. Leading through involvement, interactions, and two-way feedback is of great importance to the 9, 9 leader. The 9, 9 leader is noted not only for success and for producing results consistently; this leader also is noted as supportive both to employees and to colleagues, according to Blake and Mouton.

Mable K. Staupers, an African American woman and founder of the crusade for the employment and integration of Negro nurses in the armed services, has a leadership style that resembles Blake and Mouton's 9, 9 leader.

Staupers challenged the upper echelons of the U.S. Army and Navy and insisted that each branch accept black women nurses in the military nurses' corps during World War II (Franklin, 1982). She secured grants to build a permanent headquarters for the National Association of Colored Graduate Nurses (NACGN) at Rockefeller Center and achieved results that influenced the African American community.

Blake and Mouton (1985) suggested that the "processes of leadership are involved in achieving results with and through others" (p. 196). These processes aid in developing the leader as well as employees, allowing all to succeed. Consistent feedback to employees is just as important as consistent feedback to the leader. Leaders who strive to balance concern for production and concerns for people are more apt to develop optimum results through employee participation.

Summary

In order to develop a great leader, core element, traits, and processes must be identified. Although the definition of leadership is as diverse as the theorists who focus on the ideal leadership model, all would agree that the success of a leader is based upon consistent results. The researcher has provided an exploration of six leadership theories that included key processes as well as traits of leaders. When revisiting the thought of what makes a good leader, the answer is a combination of Blanchard and Johnson's (1985), Bass and Stogdill's (1990), Maxwell's (1993), Burns's (2003), Greenleaf's (2002), and Blake and Mouton's (1985) theories. The beauty of leadership is in identifying and activating the balance between each theory to create success for the organization and success for the followers. The art of mastering each is contingent on the values, morals, and beliefs of the leaders. Leadership skills are just as important as leadership behaviors; one of the major objectives is to learn how to balance both to motivate others.

Motivation Theories

The study of human behavior has been a challenge for theorists throughout the years. Maslow (1978), Vroom (1995), McClelland and Winter (1969), Herzberg (1997), Alderfer (Miner, 2002), and Adams (1963) initiated their research with the question of what makes people do the things they do. Why do some humans consistently succeed while others fail? Is motivation an internal or an external force? What effect does motivation have on behavior? The answers to these questions are just as complex as the questions themselves.

This literature review explores intrinsic and extrinsic motivation and the impact each has upon the needs, expectancy, and equity theory of motivation. It analyzes and compares needs theories such as Maslow's (1987), Alderfer's (Miner, 2002), Herzberg's (1997), McClelland and Winter's (1969) with process theories such as Vroom's (1995) expectancy theory and Adams' (1963) equity theory. This researcher explored the foundation and articulation of the needs, process, and reinforcement theories to establish a baseline of what motivates the behavior of human beings. This researcher analyzed the differing paradigms of motivation in order to identify what motivates African American women to become leaders in American corporations.

Motivation

Vroom (1995) defined motivation as a process that invokes choices among work roles in order to encourage satisfaction and to enhance performance or effectiveness. Motivation in the work atmosphere differs from the level of motivation within relationships, according to Vroom. Motivation is the driving force in the choices that humans make to obtain satisfaction and to meet expected results. Motivation is what makes each person wake up every day and travel to his or her place of employment regardless of the weather, date, or current state of being. Herzberg (1997) explained motivation as the force behind the means of the intangible human nature. Motivation is the part of the human spirit that is less likely to be seen, but often heard and displayed.

Although strategies may differ, the objective to achieve remains constant with motivated people. Results are a motivational factor for some, while the act of completion is a factor for others (Herzberg, 1997). In the framework of motivation, human beings are motivated by internal or external factors. As such, motivational factors may be as perpetual as change within a lifetime. Motivational factors may be as diverse as the various breeds of animals, plants, and insects, meaning that several processes motivate humans.

Maslow (1987) defined motivation as a "parental impulse" (p. 174) that guides humans to their destiny, objectives, and purposes in life and as a yearning that must be satisfied through the satisfaction of needs. He viewed motivation as an appetite and a longing to be more and to achieve more.

Motivational Factors

According to Herzberg (1997), humans are motivated by an assortment of factors. Fulfillment and psychological development is a result of motivational factors. Motivational factors are the conditions or things that prompt people to action. Tangible factors such as wages, pension, and good working conditions motivate humans.

Many who are motivated by tangible factors, will increase or decrease performance by positive or negative amounts. Others may be motivated by intangible motivational factors such as respect, a sense of value, or consistent work environment challenges. Humans motivated by intangible factors are motivated by feelings and perceptions (Herzberg). These perceptions are reality within the minds of the motivated or unmotivated.

Motivational factors are the intrinsic or extrinsic elements that initiate the behavior that produces change (Vroom, 1995). These factors are described as transitioning from Point A to Point B of a situation.

Recognizing that humans are motivated by an array of motivational factors, distinguishing intrinsic from extrinsic motivation is optimal to answer the question of what motivates human beings.

Intrinsic/Extrinsic Motivation

As noted by Maslow (1987), intrinsic motivation is an internal state that activates the behavior, yearning, or influences that initiates change within a being. The motivational factors are internal and are not changed or altered by external factors. Intrinsic motivational factors are influenced by the body, mind, spirit, and soul. Humans respond to the things they find pleasurable. The desire to drink water is initiated by the intrinsic motivator of thirst. When one is hot, the intrinsic motivator of finding a cool place may encourage one to go into an air-conditioned facility. Fatigue tends to alert the intrinsic motivator mechanism of finding a place to rest, such as a bed, couch, or chair. These motivators are innate and evolve from within human beings.

Behaviors, changes, and influences controlled by external factors are extrinsic motivators. Vroom (1995) suggested that money, rewards, perks, and insurance are examples of extrinsic motivators. Human beings are taught the value of external motivation factors, thus indicating that extrinsic motivators are flexible and unpredictable within each individual's definition of worth or meaning. A person running a marathon is motivated extrinsically to win the gold medal. When a college student consistently attends class and pays tuition, the extrinsic motivation is a college degree. External rewards are the motivating factors in extrinsic motivation, as the power of influence and persuasion continues to fascinate the human mind. The old theory of mind over matter becomes a reality and humans are more apt to focus on the reward rather than on the performance required to accomplish the reward.

Herzberg's (1997) and Vroom's (1995) theories debate over the influence of intrinsic verses extrinsic motivational factors. To believe that humans learn motivational factors during childhood assumes that motivation is not an innate behavior (Vroom). Another theory is

Motivating Change

that motivation is a learned behavior that may be altered, enhanced, or changed throughout the status of life (Herzberg). This writing will analyze the beliefs of Adam's (1963) equity theory, Vroom's expectancy theory, and Maslow's (1987), McClelland and Winter's (1969), and Herzberg's needs theory.

Process Theories

Process theorists examine processes that influence behaviors among human beings. Vroom's (1995) expectancy theory and Adam's (1963) equity theory are two examples of process theories. The baseline of the expectancy theory is that motivation is initiated by the belief that a particular behavior will produce a desired outcome (Vroom). The core of the equity theory is input and output. According to the equity theory, there is a fair balance between the input such as skills and performance of employees and the outputs such as salary, rewards, and benefits provided to an employee. According to Adams, the balance of input and output is believed to motivate humans.

Adam's Theory

Adam's (1963) equity theory showed that a perceived balance between inputs and outputs motivates human performance. Inputs are tangible or intangible items or behaviors provided to acquire a specific output. Skills, commitment, determination, confidence, teamwork, loyalty, and endeavor are examples of inputs. According to Adams, outputs usually are financial rewards or intangible emotional benefits that are obtained from an input. Outputs include salary, commission, responsibility, training development, sense of achievement, and advancement. Inequity occurs when a person compares himself or herself with another person and believes their inputs equal the outputs of that person. When employees perceive they are getting less output for the same input as colleagues, the results will be demotivation or the exploration of other opportunities outside of the organization.

The conception of equity within human behavior promotes consistent fairness and integrity, which enhances productivity and performance (Adams, 1963). When inequity emerges, performance, productivity, and the will to fight begin to decrease. Within a relationship, each partner is committed to provide a balance between input and output. When this balance is not equal, the partner who is giving more and receiving less tends to gravitate to the less productive end of the spectrum, in order to maintain equality within the relationship. The partner who is inputting less and receiving more inadvertently will begin to give more to maintain the balance within the relationship. Adams suggested that humans are pleased when there is an equal balance of input and output in a relationship.

According to Adams (1963), employers will notice less productivity, increased absenteeism, and rapid turnover when employees feel that the balance within the workplace is in favor of the company. Monetary rewards, benefits, and self-achievement within an organization measure employees' output. Input must constantly equal output for employees to feel a sense of fairness within the workplace. Adams also believed that if output were greater than input, employees would perform at an elevated level in order to stabilize the balance between output and input. Herzberg's (1997) needs theory differs from Adam's equity theory in the level of equity. The needs theory, according to Herzberg, associates satisfaction with accomplishment and development instead of the balance between input and output.

Vroom's Theory

Vroom's (1995) expectancy theory assumes that motivation is determined not by intrinsic factors but by extrinsic factors. Desire is obtained via motivational factors based upon the achievement of projected satisfaction or dissatisfaction. Humans join specific religious congregations based on the belief that membership will enhance their status within the community. In the workforce, employees produce quality and timely work because of the confidence that promotion is based upon performance and effectiveness. Partnerships are established and maintained due to the presumed benefits of the shareholders. Expected gains outweigh assumed losses; therefore, business relationships are necessary due to the anticipated value.

Vroom's (1995) expectancy theory provides a concrete analysis of pain versus pleasure. It is based upon three beliefs: valence, expectancy, and force. Valence is identified as the value placed upon the incentive or reward. Vroom identifies two expectancies: the expectancy that effort will lead to performance (E-P), and the expectancy that performance will lead to outcomes one wants (P-O).

Vroom (1995) defines valence as "an affective orientations toward particular outcomes" (p. 18). Positive valence is an outcome that a human prefers to acquire rather than not to acquire. A positive valence is placed upon working through the resignation period. A zero valence is identified when an outcome does not have a tangible value to the person. The ability to acquire or not to acquire creates an unconcerned notion within the person. An outcome has a negative valence when the person chooses not to acquire rather than to acquire the reward. When maintaining the status quo becomes more pleasurable than striving to succeed, the outcome has negative valence.

Human motivation is guided by motives, the perceived reward for performance. Vroom (1995) defined motives, believed to be positive and negative, as predilection outcomes. Positive motives correlate with positive valences, and negative motives correlate with negative valances. A zero valence may signify the neutrality of motives, indicating indifferent values and outcomes. Positive motives and valence are viewed as desirable, appealing, or interesting to the respondent, whereas negative motives or valences are viewed as undesirable, uninteresting, or unappealing.

According to the expectancy theory, the five properties of work roles are "to provide financial remuneration, require the expenditure of energy, involve the production of goods and services, permit or require social interaction, affect the social status of the worker" (Vroom, 1995, p. 51). The opinions regarding the impact of finances among theorists vary greatly. Although some people consider money to answer all things, money also is the resource needed to secure basic needs (Vroom). Salary, wages, and incentives also are used to acquire retirement plans, healthcare, and social activities. However, millions of financially independent humans continue to work to attain an outcome that is far greater than money. Although finances may be a motivational factor for some, Vroom recognized that money is not a motivational factor for all humans.

In comparison, Adams' (1963) equity theory equated money as a motivational factor for humans seeking employment. Employees work (input) to obtain salary or wages (output). The work performance has a direct impact on the salary or wages earned when comparing the equity theory with the expectancy theory. Therefore, managers may amplify the level of motivation among employees by tailoring rewards, incentives, and benefits to the desires and expectations of employees.

Vroom (1995) suggested that when an increased amount of energy is used to acquire an outcome, positive valence is attached to the achievement. However, when an intensified amount of energy expenditure generates negative results, the valence is focused on the energy and not on the reward. The value changes rapidly to an area that may denote successful reward and achievement.

According to Vroom (1995), the collaboration of energy expenditure and the desire to serve a purpose and to achieve goals introduces the motive of production for goods and services. People strive to discover, to understand, and to fulfill their goal, destiny, and enrichment of life. There always should be an end to a means, which extrinsically motivates thousands in search of outcomes. The reward of completion and accomplishment not only boost morale but also serve a moral purpose of justification.

People are motivated when a reward satisfies a specific need or value, when a favorable balance between efforts and execution is accomplished, or when a positive perception equates to a perceived reward (Vroom, 1995). Another extrinsic reward is social status and social interaction. Developed relationships single-handedly have motivated millions to remain in a work environment that no longer satisfies needs. The pain of terminating lifelong relationships becomes a motive to continue to stay at a particular employment facility. This belief has a direct relationship with Maslow's (1987) theory, as it identifies establishing and maintaining relationships as being an essential asset of motivational factors among humans.

Expectancy, which Vroom (1995) rates in strengths, is the belief that a particular input produces a particular outcome. It is created by the belief that an objective or activity is capable of being completed. Maximal strength or effort will produce results, whereas minimum strength or efforts will not. Unlike Adams' (1963) theory of equity defining input equals output, Vroom denotes that if diminutive efforts are input, no outcome will emerge. Expectancy is the basis of one's perceptions, which equates to reality within each human belief. If perception is perceived to be truth and believing is seeing externally, than motivation is an extrinsic factor.

Outcomes are achieved by controllable and uncontrollable selections. For example, a person playing the slot machine in Las Vegas is not sure that he or she will win the grand prize. The act of winning is strictly by chance due to uncontrollable factors and means unannounced to the person. Although the person may believe winning will be the outcome, there is no guarantee. Similar is the chance that a person may take during an interview for a promotion. Although the person may believe that they are the most qualified of the applicants, their selection is based upon uncontrollable factors.

Vroom (1995) stated, "whenever an individual chooses between an alternative that involves uncertain outcomes, it seems clear that his behavior is affected not only by his preferences among these outcomes but also by the degree to which he believes these outcomes to be probable" (p. 20). Individualized expectancy is based upon current situations and probabilities. The presumption within any mechanism is the ability to increase or decrease a human's level of motivation. The important aspect is the ability to observe the level of value that is placed upon the perceived reward.

Vroom (1995) stated that force or instrumentality is the probability that certain actions will produce a particular outcome. Vroom's modularization of the expectancy theory indicates that V = valence outcome and E = the strength of the expectancy. Therefore (VE) = motivation, to provide a summation of the expectancy theory. However, positive or negative, valence has minimal impact upon the outcome, except where the valence is zero. Whereas the force of expectancy provides a direct relationship in the probability that the outcome will occur, a zero valence of outcome or expectancy will exemplify a zero force.

If expectancy is reaching far into the future, the force needed to reach positive outcomes must be positive, according to Vroom (1995). Therefore, positive energy would influence positive valence and the probability of success would be more achievable. This rationale is what encourages humans to think beyond the visual necessities and to focus on the future aspects of the outcomes, which is ultimately the motivational factor.

Vroom (1995) concluded that there is a direct correlation between ability and motivation. This belief assumes that humans are motivated to do the things within their own performance capability. Accordingly, assigning a particular task within the scope of an employee's spectrum of training would generate stronger levels of motivation due to a positive expected outcome. The positive numerical valence would therefore induce a positive force to achieve the task due to realistic outcomes. This scenario provides the hypothetical conclusion of the ability to achieve in areas where success is realistic and attainable, increasing the level of expectancy due to controllable means.

Another assumption about motivation is that employees appreciate consistent information about abilities, as indicated by Vroom (1995). This means that 360 degree concrete feedback may enhance motivation among employees when provided on a regular basis. Identifying expectations and areas of strengths and weakness may trigger explorations of creative venues to succeed. Employees are able to improve areas of opportunity for growth and challenge in order to increase performance.

The final assumption regarding motivation is that employees prefer positive to negative feedback. Awareness of proficient and deficient areas identifies areas of opportunity and may become a motivational factor. Many employees increase performance after disciplinary action, whereas others display a decrease in performance. Vroom (1995) believes that motivation is activated by expectancy that is driven from pain versus pleasure perception of each human being.

Needs Theories

Needs are believed to be the initial motivator that change human behavior, according to Maslow (1987). The need to have, attain, or acquire will induce the behavior that will prompt, drive, or enforce change to occur. A need is described as an element that necessitates the attention, action, or obligation of one's attention, mindset, or ability (Maslow). Although needs may vary and change throughout one's lifetime, basic needs remain constant.

When analyzing the needs theory, there are five prominent thought leaders: Herzberg (1997), McClelland and Winter (1969), Alderfer (Miner, 2002), and Maslow (1987). Although each theorist has his own unique approach and methodology, the foundation and framework of the theories focus on the correlation of needs and motivation. Herzberg compartmentalizes motivation into a two-factor theory: hygiene and motivation factors. Although both are essential, Herzberg isolated the causation of dissatisfaction and satisfaction within the workforce. Herzberg listed working conditions, quality of supervision, salary, employment, and security as hygiene factors. Motivational factors, according to Herzberg, include achievement, recognition, growth and development, and interest in a job.

McClelland and Winter (1969) believed that the need to achieve is a predominant motivator of human beings and people who are constantly trying to better themselves are motivated by the need to achieve. Maslow's hierarchy of needs identified strategies that may increase motivation in order to understand the basic concept of human behavior.

Herzberg's Theory

Herzberg (1997) believed that the extrinsic factors of a position promote dissatisfaction within the workforce. This thought pattern is the total opposite of Vroom's (1995) theory, which indicated that the extrinsic factors are a vital part of motivation, and that motivation supports satisfaction within the workforce. These extrinsic factors produce a negative environment but do not have a direct attachment to the level of motivation displayed by a person. Therefore, Herzberg believed that extrinsic factors can create dissatisfaction but will not create satisfaction that will evolve into motivation or a motivational factor. He described hygiene factors as the extrinsic factors that yield a positive work environment.

As indicated by Herzberg (1997), working conditions, salary, security, interpersonal relations, supervision, and position-created status are examples of hygienes. The absence or inadequacies of any of these areas have the ability to produce job dissatisfaction (i.e., hygiene). However, increasing the amount of hygienes will not affect the level of performance. An example would be increasing the salary of a poor performing employee in order to increase the level of production. The employee's performance will remain the same no matter how significant the salary is adjusted.

Herzberg (1997) equated hygiene in theory to hygiene in the natural sciences by associating the definition to health. Hygienes in a work environment ensure a healthy and safe workplace in the mental, physical, and behavior aspects of one's state. Ensuring hygienes is a preventive measure within the work environment.

The variance between Herzberg's (1997) theory and Adam's (1963) equity theories is the lack of the initiative to attempt to establish or maintain balance between input and output of outcomes. An employee influenced by the equity motivational theory would increase the level of performance to compensate for the increase in salary. According to Vroom's (1995) expectancy theory, this same employee would increase the level of performance with the expected probability of receiving another increase in pay or another form of benefit or incentive.

Unlike hygienes factors, motivators are intrinsic factors that enhance satisfaction, as noted by Herzberg (1997). Motivator factors, also identified as job enhancement factors, include achievement, recognition, relationship, responsibility, and advancement and growth. This feeling of achievement and accomplishment not only changes the attitude of humans but also provides job satisfaction and self-actualization.

When humans develop the need for fulfillment, the drive to continue and to press beyond present obstacles begins to emerge (Herzberg, 1997). This drive is evident when discussing the need to complete college to a student in the final year of undergraduate education. The drive of completion for graduating students is extremely persistent, even if it means studying several hours after midnight. The need to achieve the objective successfully becomes more demanding than the need to obtain eight hours of sleep.

In order for recognition to have meaning within the workplace, employees must receive truthful feedback. People respond and reply to direct, constructive feedback. Employees enjoy praise and acknowledgment when it is a direct and factual response to performance (Herzberg, 1997). Vroom (1995) pointed out the same pattern. Job satisfaction incorporates the pros and cons of the work atmosphere and the employees' ability to execute. Reinforcement of performance promotes higher aspirations to achieve, which is an indispensable motivation factor.

One of the similarities between the theories of Vroom (1995) and Herzberg (1997) is the connection between job satisfaction and relationship. Both theories identified client relationships as a driving force of satisfaction within the service industry. Vroom suggested that people who acquired wealth would continue to work at their current place of employment in order to maintain relationships. Herzberg made the same distinct observation in the association between client relationship and motivation. In fact, he suggested that one of the core elements of motivation is the client relationship. This is often is seen in the sales field when salespeople remain within a territory for years due to the concrete friendships established among customers. These solid friendships support consistently strong sales results.

Herzberg (1997) suggested that self-scheduling, authority to communicate, control of resources, and accountability are aspects of responsibility. Responsibility correlated with identifying and meeting customer's needs, managing assets, and following the established protocol. Depending on the level of responsibility, the integrity of motivation may enhance the employee's performance due to the expectation of greater responsibility within the workplace.

The last aspect of Herzberg's (1997) motivators is advancement and growth; in today's society, this translates into growth and development. It is in this area that many corporations identify the employees' expectations of the company. Career outlooks have the ability to influence performance directly as a motivating factor. The opportunity to learn and to grow within a work environment may enhance job satisfaction, loyalty, and endurance. Some examples of advancement and growth are career succession discussions and online career assessment tools that assist in discovering growth opportunities within an organization and in identifying future opportunities.

To identify the preferred work attitude, the appropriate incentive must be provided. Herzberg (1997), like Maslow (1987), identified self-actualization as an essential ingredient in formulating positive attitudes. In simple terms, the need to relate to one's inimitable, ingenious, self-reliant being in a positive formation has a bonding impact on attitude within the workplace (Herzberg). This poses the question in relation to motivation. Attitude affects outlook, and outlook affects the level of motivation within each human being. If a person is unable to visualize success, they are not motivated to attain any element of success or improvement.

As the hygiene factors are satisfied, the motivators will address the needs that are necessary to enhance performance. The interesting aspect concerning motivators is the direct impact the status of the hygiene factors has upon the development of the motivators. The hygiene factors are essential to job satisfaction but are not essential to motivation (Herzberg, 1997). According to Adam's (1963) equity theory, humans are in search of fairness. This same search for fairness is evident when addressing the hygiene factors. Job fairness is accomplished through hygiene factors. Once baseline job satisfaction is achieved via hygiene factors, the avenues leading to motivation can be identified.

Motivation, according to Herzberg (1997), is achieved when the appropriate incentive is identified and supplied. The fundamental element of motivation is self-respect and respect of others. A consistency of reverence of performance, attitude, and behavior promotes the desire to give and to do more for further recognition. Although monetary incentives are listed as job satisfiers once fairness is achieved, production is not connected to the level or amount of financial incentives. Therefore, salary remains in the category of hygiene factors.

Motivation is a derivative of recognition, achievement, relationship, and growth potential. Alter the areas that influence behaviors, and the level of motivation will reflect the alteration. According to Herzberg (1997), motivation is influenced by intrinsic factors and is evolved within the innate aspect of the being and the extrinsic probabilities. Study the innate behavior to identify the areas of importance to a person, and the motivational factors and areas of influence will be evident.

McClelland and Winter's Theory

McClelland and Winter's (1969) theory of motivation is similar to Maslow's (1987) and Herzberg's (1997) in its systematic approach and importance placed upon achievement as a learned motivational factor. This theory derives from the belief that motivation is a learned behavior that can be altered by environments, patterns, and mental alterations. In early childhood, a child's learning new phrases yields praises from adults; therefore, the babblings of an infant become a sure sign of growth. This same child, during the toddler years, is rewarded for learning how to go to the potty independently, yet another form of achievement that constitutes praise from parents. During the school age years, this adolescent is rewarded for successfully completing grammar school, high school, and then college. All three degrees signify achievement and accomplishments in life. According to McClelland and Winter (1969), the question is what is the motive that encourages the need to achieve.

McClelland and Winter (1969) identified motives as groups of expectancies with a common level of importance to an individual. This level of importance is measured in strengths; once the magnitude of the strength is defined, the essential element of the motive is acknowledged. This approach is noted when a candidate is running for a political office. Many people run to increase notoriety within the community; others run to obtain victory. Once the strength of the motive is identified, the actual element of motivation is made known, which ultimately reveals the motivational factor. For some, the motivational factor of running during a campaign is the achievement and acquisition of a political position; for others, it may be recognition among peers. Conceptualizing the motive will reveal the learned aspect of motivation within human development and will provide a great opportunity for intrinsic change within the level of expectancy.

If change is constant, then the evolution of motivation also is constant. Studying motivation as a learned behavior would mean that motivation is different within each human being based upon learned conditions. McClelland and Winter (1969) concluded that achievement, self-actualization, goal setting, and interpersonal supports could be changed via the learning environment, such as a class.

Similar to Maslow's (1987) and Herzberg's (1997), McClelland and Winter's (1969) theory is conceptualized by needs. These needs are the need for achievement, the need for power, and the need for affiliation.

Motivating Change

The need for achievement is the strongest of the three objectives and, therefore, the essential need among humans. McClelland and Winter suggested that the need to succeed is an innate behavior within the human population. Achievers tend to set goals and to achieve goals. Achievers focus on success instead of kickbacks and monetary incentives. Achievers are motivated by the ability to achieve within any given environment. If the ability to achieve is eradicated, the achiever is no longer motivated.

McClelland and Winter (1969) motivational theory of achievement is similar to Vroom's (1995) expectancy theory of motivation. However, McClelland and Winter's primary focus was motivation through achievement. In both theories, the person's expectation must be realistic to trigger any characteristics of motivation. If the expectancy or probabilities are not obtainable, the level of motivation is nearly obsolete. However, if the expectancy or achievement is attainable, the level of motivation increases within the person. This synopsis identifies a direct correlation between motivation and realistic expectation. If a team believes that winning a tournament is realistic, the level of motivation will move into the direction of success. In this case, seeing is believing and believing is achieving, when achieving is the motivational factor creating the action within a person's mindset.

McClelland and Winter (1969) identified power as the second motivator of humans. People who are motivated by power enjoy control. Power- motivated humans are characterized as dominate, strong-willed, and authoritative. This group's focal motive is to dictate and to govern others. In American corporations, this person's profession might be law enforcement, judicial, a military officer, or a public official. People who are motivated by power tend to be non-risk takers; part of their motivation is the ability to take credit for achievements. Power- motivated people are outcome driven when the success provides self-recognition.

McClelland and Winter (1969) stated that people who are motivated by power strive to be influential and impactful in achieving results. These groups also are noted to be over achievers when pursuing success and fulfilling challenges. The power driven are extremely outspoken and strive to be well-established leaders among peer groups. Those who are motivated by power usually live self-controlled lives with boundaries that are clearly defined. The level of perceived power obtainable within a situation strictly controls the level of motivation of the power driven. Less motivation is given to areas in which the power driven begins to blend within the group, such as in group presentations and teambuilding activities.

In a relationship, the power- driven person presents as being dogmatic and self-centered, according to McClelland and Winter (1969). This person tends to function better with a companion that is more passive and timid. The dominant mate makes all of the decisions in the relationship, whereas the less aggressive mate operates in a more submissive role. An intimate relationship with a power driven person can be successful as long as each partner has a clear understanding of roles and expectations.

The third area of needs motivation is the need for affiliation. Humans need to feel a sense of belonging or association to others (McClelland & Winter, 1969). This area correlates with Herzberg's (1997) hygiene as a need for relationship. Humans who are motivated by affiliation need team projects and group settings to feel as if they are contributing to the success of the organization. Their mindset is usually one of succeeding or failing together as a unit instead of as various parts. Interpersonal relationships are very important to the affiliation-motivated person. In relationship formation and the area of courtship, the affiliation-motivated tends to value the importance of family structure and the unit of the family. In a marriage, this group strives very hard to maintain a long-lasting marriage with the emphasis on teamwork and partnership.

McClelland and Winter (1969) provided some enlightening points on the various areas of importance within a human's mindset, as well as on how these areas serve as motivators. According to these theorists, achievement is a key motivator of human behavior. They believed that human motivation is a learned intrinsic factor that can be altered via a change in the thinking pattern of humans. Finally, McClelland and

Winter stressed the importance of direct and precise feedback as a means of motivating.

Maslow's Theory

One of the most prominent theorists of all time is Maslow, the creator of the Hierarchy of Needs. Maslow's (1987) Needs theory addresses the five essential needs of every human in accordance to the level of importance, termed *prepotency*. The five needs that Maslow believed motivate humans are physiological, safety belonging esteem and self-actualization. The lower level needs must be reasonably satisfied for a person to move to the next level of needs. Physiological needs address the backbones of needs both by providing homeostasis and by satisfying individualized appetites (Maslow, 1987). Maslow's physiological needs, although identified as the baseline of motivation, are equivalent in theory to Herzberg's (1997) hygiene factors. The physiological needs include nutrition, air, intimacy, and sleep; when the physiological needs are not met, the body immediately develops a craving for these needs. Once physiological needs are successfully fulfilled, humans are able to focus on another level of needs. However, before obtaining physiological needs, human behaviors and efforts are focused on meeting these fundamental needs. Therefore, physiological needs are motivation factors that necessitate the attention and efforts of humans.

Maslow (1987) indicated that bringing order to chaos is the essence of the second tier of needs, safety needs. Security, order, limits, dependency, protection, and structure are elements of the safety needs. These areas of development emerge when danger or transition is present. After a human finds nourishment for the body, the desire for nourishment of the mind becomes crucial. Food for the mind is inner peace, joy, happiness, and wholeness. The search for completeness will send the mind into a radical motivation mode (Maslow). Maslow's theory equates to Adam's (1963) belief concerning humans' desire to maintain equity within a relationship. Humans need to maintain safety to achieve holistic balance.

Safety needs also include the need for structure and order within one's life. The need to have a solid foundation of spiritual beliefs motivates humans to join religious organizations. Many develop morals and beliefs as well as individualized order based upon denominational doctrines. Developing a spiritual lifestyle also provides a sense of security that aids in eliminating the fears and anxieties of humans by putting their trust in a higher being. Thousands of humans are motivated to attend churches and synagogues weekly because of the yearning to fulfill safety needs (Maslow, 1987). Vroom's (1997) theory of expectancy addressed this same need of fulfillment by concluding that many humans attend church and synagogues with the expectancy of obtaining structure, peace, and balance within their lives.

The need to belong or to feel love is a yearning that many humans experience throughout the stages of life, according to Maslow (1987). Examples include a recent divorcee searching for an opportunity to love again, and a child on his first day at a new school longing to establish friendship and associations. Maslow's third tier of hierarchy is evidenced by the human nature to be married, to have children, to join clubs, and to develop friendships.

Belonging and loving is an interactive need, which means that the level of motivation is based upon the ability to give and to receive love, affection, affiliation, and companionship. A complete person operating in wholeness is aware of the need to maintain balance within the area of belonging and love. The chief motivator for humans in the third tier of needs is the desire to achieve. This urge to achieve will not be satisfied unless the relationship is obtained.

The fourth tier of Maslow's (1987) needs theory is esteem needs, which are categorized as strength or prestige. Humans are motivated by the potential ability to attain self-respect and the respect of others. The mirror reflection is just as important as the naked eye view of one's characteristic, traits, and being. Esteem as it relates to strengths includes success, sufficiency, proficiency, confidence, and independence. During the fourth tier, purpose, destiny, and life objectives are pronounced.

After humans explore their surroundings and find a healthy median, an exploration of the inner person begins. The motivation derives from obtaining equilibrium between the inner and outer aspects of individuality.

Maslow (1987) indicated that the second aspect of the esteem need is prestige, the need to be regarded with high esteem. Not only do humans sense the need to be self-praised, but they also need to feel admired by others. Achievement of the esteem needs provides internal confidence, value, and adequacy.

Self-actualization is the fifth and final tier of Maslow's (1987) hierarchy of motivation needs. Recognized as the top of the mountain, self-actualization is the push to excel in life and the drive to move toward success and fulfillment. Maslow expressed the importance of satisfying the previous four areas of needs to be able to recognize the void in self-actualization. It is debatable whether every human is able to reach this area of need. For many, it is described as an endless search for one's self and purpose.

Maslow (1987) also argued that identifying purpose in life is an endless journey that must be traveled with patience and endurance. Life is filled with rapid transition and swift change; the goal to achieve is the motivational factor of self-actualization. No one wants to live a defeated life without destiny, purpose, or mission. In self-actualization, the motivation is to be complete in pursuing purpose.

Alderfer's Theory

According to Miner (2002), Alderfer developed the existence, relatedness, and growth (ERG) theory to address inadequacies that are noted in many of the needs hierarchy formulations. The ERG theory assumed that human activity is motivated specifically by needs. These needs are subdivided into three categories according to importance. Similar to Maslow's (1987) theory, Alderfer's theory states that humans must meet the need of the most important group before energy and effort and can be devoted to the needs of the second group. Similarly the needs of the first and second groups must be met before meeting the needs of the third group.

Also similar to Maslow's (1987) theory, Alderfer's theory is in a three tier pyramidal form, with existence needs at the base of the pyramid. Existence needs, according to Alderfer, included the fundamentals of life such as food, water, air, clothing safety, physical love, and affection. "The less existence needs are satisfied, the more they will be desired" (Miner, 2002, p. 142). This statement is parallel to Maslow's theory. Also similar to Maslow's theory, Alderfer's theory stated that the more existence needs are satisfied, the more second tier needs will be desired.

The second tier of needs is relatedness, which includes the need to be recognized, to feel secure and to be part of a group, family, and culture, is recognized as Maslow's need to belong and to be loved. "The less relatedness needs are satisfied, the more existence needs will be desired" (Miner, 2002, p. 142). Baumeister and Leary (1995) introduced the need to belong as a goal-directed function designed to initiate satisfaction. This need may be transferable from one being to another without limitations or restrictions. The need to belong is a powerful desire that is centered within the inner most aspect of one's soul. As the desire for relatedness needs decrease, the need for the third tier needs will increase.

Growth needs are Alderfer's third tier needs and encompass self-development, competency, and potential. "The more growth needs are satisfied, the more they will be desired" (Miner, 2002, p. 142). The growth need is similar to Maslow's self-actualization level. This area of motivation challenges employees to be the best they can be by using their instinctual abilities to succeed (Maslow, 1987). Self-development or self-actualization is seen when employees are encouraged to career plan to establish career goals for the next 12 months to five years. Employees then must design training programs that are favorable to the career development strategy. This challenge encourages employees to think outside of the box to become successful, and to create an atmosphere that is conducive to learning new things daily. According to Maslow (1987), self-actualization or self-development challenges employees to strive to reach their destiny and purpose in life without limits.

Alderfer's theory suggests that humans are energized or motivated when they identify an unsatisfied need. Once they satisfy a need, humans transition to other areas of unsatisfied needs (Miner, 2002). In Maslow's (1987) theory, lower-level needs, such as existence needs and love or belonging needs, must be satisfied before higher-level needs, such as esteem needs and self actualization, can be satisfied. An exception to both Maslow's and Alderfer's theory is that the hierarchy of needs is not necessary in a fixed order and may be altered by individual stages in life (Maslow). Therefore, motivation is visualized as a stepping-stone or a bridge to satisfying unmet needs in various stages of life.

Gagne (2005) defined needs as a universal necessity that provides the nourishment to promote human growth and development. A need is satisfied when the finished product promotes psychological health and well-being. This belief of self-determination and autonomy flows very well with the beliefs of Maslow's (1987), McClelland and Winter's (1969), Alderfer (Miner, 2002), and Herzberg's (1997) needs theories. The desire to satisfy is believed to be the motivational factor in fulfilling unmet needs regardless of the stage of life or development.

Another view of the needs theory is that humans identify their needs, attempt to meet their needs, and then fulfill their needs through various aspects of motivation, which starts the cycle over again by identifying another aspect of unmet needs (Halepota, 2005). This belief, which is similar to the needs theories of Maslow, McClelland and Winter, Alderfer, and Herzberg, suggests that motivation is a consistent, continuous part of the psychological needs of achievement and accomplishment. Based on this concept, humans will maintain a level of motivation due to their desire to fulfill a need. Therefore, as long as a desire is present, the person will continue to be motivated to fulfill the unmet need.

Reinforcement Theory

B. F. Skinner (1953) developed the reinforcement theory, which proposed that the effects of the consequences of a particular behavior would feed back into the organism, known as operant conditioning, the foundation of his theory. There are four types of operant condition: positive reinforcement, negative reinforcement, extinction, and punishment. Positive reinforcement is administering a reward following a behavior, thereby increasing that behavior.

The second operant condition, negative reinforcement, also strengthens behaviors. Negative reinforcement is the removal of negative conditions or stressors as a consequence to a behavior. An example of a negative reinforcement is having the title "rookie" removed from a new manager when the sales team achieves its 100 percent quota. The removal of the negative verbiage reinforces the behavior. Therefore, negative reinforcement is the removal of negative connotations or stimuli as a result of behavior, according to Skinner (1953).

Extinction, which weakens a behavior, is the third operant behavior. When reinforcement is not provided through rewards or withdrawals, the behavior stops; the definition of extinction. During extinction, nothing is provided as a consequence of the behavior (Dunn, 2002). This behavior is observed when employees volunteer for special assignments and do not obtain rewards or recognition for the work completed. When the next opportunity to volunteer is presented, the employees decline as a result of extinction.

Another weakening behavior is punishment. During the punishment process, which is the last operant condition, a punishment is given as a consequence of the behavior. An example is an employee having his or her budget decreased for going over budget during the previous year. Punishment, similar to extinction, is designed to eradicate behavior, according to Dunn (2002).

Skinner's operant conditioning is similar to Thorndike's "law of effect, which stated that a particular behavior is stamped in when followed by certain consequences" (Skinner, 1953, p. 60). Thorndike's law of effect states that a series of responses can be linked together to satisfy an objective that will bring frustration if not accomplished. The law of exercises connects strengths with application and weakness when a practice is discontinued (Thorndike, 1932). Thorndike believed that learning is accomplished through effects and exercises, which are incentives and application, and learning is a result of previous encounters with stimuli.

Summary

People are motivated by a variety of elements, aspects, and factors. Motivation is individualized based on childhood experiences, environment circumstances, and incentives. When responding to what motivates African Americans in the workplace, the answer is still unclear. African Americans are motivated by a variety of elements at different stages in life. A major part of identifying the answer is to understand the history and culture of African Americans to obtain a better understanding of the needs. According to Maslow's hierarchy of needs, if the basic needs are not met, all efforts of motivation are driven to meet these needs.

CHAPTER 3: RESEARCH DESIGN METHODOLOGY

Introduction

Chapter 3 describes the research methodology, research design, data collection, sampling, and data analysis. This chapter also describes the role of the researcher in the data collection procedure, as well as the criteria for selecting participants.

The research design selected for this research was qualitative, with a phenomenological method to explore the meanings and experiences associated with what motivates African American women to lead in American corporations. Phenomenological research explores the intuitive aspects of human experiences. The use of phenomenological research was appropriate for this research as a means of understanding the patterns and themes experienced by African American women in leadership. Studies of human experiences are not approachable through quantitative research methods (Moustakas, 1994). The researcher examined what motivates African American women through life experiences shared through in-depth interviews.

Research Design

Qualitative research enables the researcher to study the natural phenomena of individuals through experiences. Creswell (1998) stated the following:

> Qualitative research is an inquiry process of understanding based on distinct methodological traditions of inquiry that explores a social or human problem. The researcher builds a complex, holistic picture, analyzes words, reports

> detailed views of informants, and conducts the study in a natural setting. (p. 15)

In qualitative research, the researcher is interested in experiences, structures, and natural activities in the lives of humans. The researcher must be committed to extensive time in the field, willing to pledge long hours to data analysis, willing to dictate long narratives from data, and open to invoke upon a changing medium (Marshall & Rossman, 1995). Qualitative research focuses on the perspective of the participants, which challenges the researcher to be objective during the analysis process.

Quantitative research differs from qualitative research in that quantitative research deals with many cases and few variables (Creswell, 1998). Qualitative research is the opposite of quantitative research, meaning that qualitative research deals with many variables and few cases. Kvale (1996) noted that "quantitative research refers to how much, how large, and quantity" (p. 67). Qualitative research refers to what kind, as it relates to the essence of a person, place, or thing (Kvale). Observations for qualitative research take place in the natural settings of participants. Philosophical assumptions develop the framework of qualitative research, with the core objective being to identify the answers to how or what types of questions (Creswell, 1998). Qualitative research design was selected for this research study as it provides a better understanding of what motivates African American women to lead in American corporations.

Biography, phenomenology, grounded theory, ethnography, and case studies are the five traditions of qualitative research (Creswell, 1998). Each tradition has a particular purpose and objective in qualitative research design. This study utilized phenomenology to explore what motivates African American women to lead in American corporations. Phenomenology describes the experiences and perceptions of participants. Hammond and colleagues (Hammond, Howarth, & Keat, 1991) stated, "phenomenology involved the description of things as one experiences them" (p. 1). One of the critical objectives of a phenomenological research is to understand the phenomenon through data collection.

The purpose of the biography tradition is to study the experiences of a particular individual. The objective of this research was to study the experiences of 16 African American women in leadership positions in American corporations; therefore, the biography tradition was not appropriate for this particular study. When a description or interpretation of cultural or social groups was desired, the ethnography tradition was utilized. The case study tradition is useful when an exploration of a bounded system or case is essential (Creswell, 1998). The final tradition, grounded theory, is designed to create or to examine a theory. The grounded theory could serve as an adjunct to the initial phenomenological research, as a means of designing or examining a specific motivational theory. The phenomenology tradition was the most appropriate method for this research because phenomenology flows "beyond the immediate experiences of meaning in order to articulate the pre-reflective level of lived meaning, to make the invisible visible" (Kvale, 1996, p. 53).

Reliability and Validity

Reliability ensures stability and consistency within a research design. Validity refers to congruence or appropriateness of the research as the study relates to the concept of the design and the purported measure of the design (Singleton & Straits, 1998). Both validity and reliability are measurements commonly observed in quantitative research. Standards of quality verification in qualitative research are similar to validity and reliability in quantitative research. In qualitative research, the term verification is used instead of validity because "verification underscores research as a distinct approach, and legitimate mode of inquiry in its own right" (Creswell, 1998, p. 201).

Standards of Quality Verification

In a phenomenological research, "the verification and standards are related to the interpretation of the research" (Creswell, 1998, p. 207). When conducting a qualitative study, eight verification procedures could be explored. Prolonged engagement and persistent observation consists of establishing trust with participants, learning new cultures, and verifying misleading information. The researcher becomes a part of the environment and group of participants in order to obtain a better understanding of their life experiences. The second method, triangulation, allows a researcher to incorporate several sources, methods, investigators, and theories. This process includes corroborating the evidence from various resources to explore perspectives. Triangulation was utilized in the current study by incorporating motivation theories. Peer review or debriefing, the third procedure, introduces an external verification of the research process by allowing peers to analyze the research.

The fourth procedure is negative case analysis, which allows the researcher to revise initial hypotheses and to eliminate outliers during the data analysis phase. Member checks, the fifth procedure, are considered the most critical technique for establishing credibility. Member checks allow participants to review results to evaluate accuracy and credibility. With the sixth procedure, clarifying research bias, the researcher identifies past experiences, bias, prejudices, and orientations that could have altered the interpretation and approach to the research. The seventh procedure is rich, thick, description, which is an in-depth description of the research, provided by the researcher, and which allows readers to transfer the findings to other settings. The final procedure is external audits, which are completed by outside auditors (Creswell, 1998). For the purpose of this research, triangulation and member checks were used as the verification procedures.

Research Questions

The research questions for this study were:
1. What factors do African American women perceive to motivate them to lead in American corporations?
2. What are some of the perceived barriers, if any, for African American women as they pursue leadership roles?

Overview of Methodology

The philosophy of phenomenology describes objects just as one experiences them and extracts philosophy from the process (Hammond et al., 1991). Husserlian, Scheutz, Berger, and Luckmann were key theorists in the development of phenomenology in the social world. In fact, Husserlian founded phenomenology, as a philosophy, during the turn of the 20th century. Phenomenology initially began with the consciousness and experiences of humans, and eventually evolved into the real world concept of human life and achievement, according to Kvale (1996).

Phenomenology is a research method when a researcher is studying the meaning of experiences of a particular individual or group of individuals (Creswell, 1998). Phenomenology is engrossed in elucidating the consciousness of humans to grasp the qualitative diversity of personal experiences of participants (Kvale, 1996). Bringing life to the perceptions, experiences, and suppressed thoughts through research is one of the characteristics of phenomenology. The researcher utilized the methodology of phenomenology to understand the perceptions of motivation among African American women in leadership roles in American corporations.

This research began with the selection of the topic of motivation, and then proceeded to the identification of an area of interest, which were the experiences of African American women in American corporations. A three-fold problem was identified: (a) the lack of African American women in leadership, (b) the lack of published information relating to motivating African American women, and (c) the lack of understanding of motivational factors relating to African American women in leadership roles. The paradigm, or the pattern of thinking of African American women, was studied to identify a basic set of beliefs, patterns, or behaviors observed in African American women in leadership positions.

Sampling

Purposive sampling and snowballing were used to recruit participants. The strategy of purposive sampling is to recognize important resources of distinction in the population and then to select a sample that mirrors this distinction (Singleton, 2005). African American women leaders were from the population that the researcher intended to mirror. Therefore, African American women in leadership roles were the foundation to the purposive sampling criteria. Snowball sampling identified additional participants. Snowball sampling is a referral system utilized to expand the number of participants within a study (Goenwald, 2004). Members of a specific targeted population were asked to identify other potential participants who met the established criteria of the research. The concept of the snowball method is that participants who meet the criteria of a particular research often know other potential participants who meet the established criteria, according to Kvale (1996).

Participants

Participants in a phenomenological study must be individuals who have experienced the phenomenon explored by the research and who can articulate their conscious experience (Creswell, 1998). Sixteen participants represent a reasonable size in a phenomenological study, according to Creswell. Creswell stated, "The important point is to describe the meaning of a small number of individuals who have experienced the phenomenon" (p. 122). Kvale (1996) noted that 16 is an adequate number of participants to interview in a phenomenological study, with a variance of 10. Therefore, for the purpose of this study, the research participants consisted of 16 African American women in leadership roles who also were a part of the National Black MBA Association. A letter was emailed to Lester McNair, the Membership Specialist, of the National Black MBA Association to obtain permission and cooperation to utilize members of the organization for the research.

At the time of the research, all participants were leaders within their respective organizations. The research participants' job titles were

CEO, president, vice president, administrator, senior administration, director, or manager. The pay, benefits, and additional compensations of the research participants varied based upon industry standards. The researcher made initial contact, via telephone and email, with each participant. A consent form was provided to each participant before the initial encounter. The consent form stated the general purpose of the study, comments about protecting confidentiality, a statement of risk, expected benefits to participant, a request for participation, and the expected time required to participate. Upon acceptance of the invitation, each participant obtained a copy of the interview protocol, via email, before the initial interview.

Interview and observational data were recorded during the scheduled interview sessions. Each participant agreed to the interview before the interviewing session via email or telephone conversation. Upon the agreement to the interview, each participant was given a copy of the interview questions for review before the interviewing process. Providing the interview questions before the interviewing process provided time for the participants to think about responses to the questions based upon previous life experiences. The interviews took place via the telephone at each participant's current place of employment or at the home office of each participant.

Instrument

Kvale (1996) stated that the researcher is the principal instrument of data collection. The researcher served as an expert on the motivation of African American female leaders due to documented experience as an African American leader, a current member of the National Black MBA association, and her knowledge of previous studies conducted on motivation. The Motivation Interview Protocol was developed by the researcher with the intent to understand what motivates African American women to lead in American corporations. The interview questions were developed to understand the experiences associated with the barriers and motivations of the participants.

Data Collection

The Role of the Researcher

The role of the researcher, as the chief investigator, was to make initial contact with the National Black MBA Association, as well as with the participants. The researcher designed the Motivation Interview Protocol, conducted the interviews, transcribed the data, analyzed the data, and summarized the results. The researcher established rapport with participants by sharing information pertaining to previous membership status with the National Black MBA Association, Inc.

Interview

An interview is an interchange of views between the researcher and the participants about a theme of mutual interest, resembling a conversation in the level of interaction. The qualitative interview is the unstructured and nonstandardized interview due to the limited amount of structured procedures (Kvale, 1996). Interview questions were structured to the personal experiences, beliefs, feelings, and perceptions of the participants. The objective of the interviewing process was to examine the daily world from the participants' points of view. Interviewing as a form of qualitative research interprets the meaning of central themes in the world of the participants, according to Kvale. The researcher selected the interview as the method of data collection in order to retrieve a large amount of information within a short timeframe. The interview also allowed the researcher to obtain an understanding of the meaning of the everyday life and activities of participants (Marshall, 1995). The interviewing process analyzed the motivation of African American women in leadership roles in American corporations.

The Motivation Interview Protocol included 15 open-ended questions that related to experience, barriers, and motivation. The Motivation Interview Protocol was one page and included demographic questions about age, race, highest level of education completed, current job title, and years in current role. All questions listed on the protocol were asked during the interviewing process. Each interview lasted approximately 30 to 45 minutes.

Interview Questions

Fifteen open-ended questions were designed to explore the experiences of the participants. The interview questions were as follows:

1. What motivated you to pursue a leadership role?
2. How would you define motivation?
3. How would you define leadership?
4. What leadership style best describes you?
5. What impact has discrimination had on your career?
6. What are some of the barriers you encountered while pursuing leadership roles in corporations?
7. Who or what is your support system?
8. How has your support system influenced your ability to become a leader?
9. What words of wisdom would you pass on to the next generation?
10. What are your greatest challenges as an African American woman in a leadership role?
11. What are your greatest rewards as an African American woman in a leadership role?
12. What impact did mentorship have on your ability to become a leader?
13. What are some of the stereotypes you encountered?
14. What are your top five motivators?
15. Are there any other comments you would like to add?

Demographics

Demographic information obtained from each participant included age, race, salary, years in current role, position title, and highest level of education obtained.

Data Storage

Each interviewing session consisted of a recording and a verbatim transcription. Each participant was assigned a code selected with an alpha character (e.g., Participant A). Each interview session was recorded on a separate cassette tape label with the participant's letter and the date on which the interview was recorded (e.g., Participant A-8-3-07). The researcher transcribed the interviews within 48 to 72 hours of the interview session, based upon the discussion between the participant and the researcher. Notes were taken during the interviewing process to indicate pauses or words of excitement. Participants received a draft copy of the interview before documentation of the research results. Participants reviewed the draft and approved the final copy prior to the documentation of the research results and discussion. The verification procedure used was member check. In this procedure, if discrepancies were noted, a follow-up communication was emailed to participants to clarify the data. All tapes, notes, and transcriptions were stored, filed and locked away, and will remain so for five years via a computer database. After five years, the researcher will destroy all information. This process was done to ensure confidentiality and comfort in conversing with participants during the interview process. The "process of preserving the data and meanings on tape and the combined transcription and preliminary analysis greatly increases the efficiency of data analysis" (Marshall, 1995, p. 110).

Data Analysis

Data analysis provides order, structure, and organization to data in order to categorize common themes and relationships among participants. Phenomenological data analysis proceeds through the methodology of reduction, the analysis of specific statements and themes, and a search for all possible meanings (Creswell, 1998). Moustakas (1994) believed that the data analysis of a phenomenological research is segregated into three phases: (a) horizonalization, (b) clusters of meanings into themes, and (c) composite textural description. Horizonalization is the division of original protocol into statements. The statements are then subdivided into clusters of meanings with parallel phenomenological concepts grouped together. The final phase involves gathering similar clusters into a composite textural description of participants' experiences.

For the purpose of this research, the researcher used Moustaka's (1994) framework of data analysis. The researcher listened to each participant's response to the interview questions and transcribed the results from the cassette tape. Files were established to organize appropriately the data before analyzing the data. The file categories included the interview protocol, email documentations, interview cassettes and transcription, and interview notes.

The researcher analyzed transcriptions several times to obtain meanings of the participants' experiences as they related to motivation to become a leader. Statements were identified to reflect each participant's experience as it relates to motivation. Each participant's statement had independent value equal to other participants. This process is called horizonalization. During the horizonalization process, highlights were made on the transcript to identify unique experiences, which aided in identifying clusters of meaning.

The participants' statements were grouped into meaning units and clustered into themes, which denoted the specific experiences identified by participants during the interviewing process. The researcher wrote a composite texture description of the participants' experiences based upon the research questions. A synopsis of patterns and themes observed from the data analysis is noted in the summary of each question, which is reported in chapter 5.

Computer data analysis, according to Creswell (1998), was utilized to help analyze large qualitative data, such as 500 or more pages, or 20-30 interviews. NVIVO is a computer program designed to analyze phenomenological research. Some advantages of this and similar computer programs include: (a) organized storage and filing system, (b) the ability to locate material easily, (c) and more in-depth understanding of word interpretations (Creswell). Some disadvantages of using a computer program to analyze data are: (a) the researcher must learn how to operate the program, (b) computer programs may limit the researcher's ability to analyze carefully the data, (c) and limited assistance in qualitative analysis and writing narratives is provided from computer programs (Creswell). Due to the limited assistance in qualitative analysis and writing narratives, as well as a smaller sample size (i.e., 16 participants), the researcher decided not to utilize a computer program to analyze the data for this research.

Ethical Protection

An electronic request to the Institutional Review Board (IRB) for Approval to Conduct Research was submitted to Dr. David Banner, the committee chair. The IRB was submitted to ensure that ethical standards were met prior to conducting the research. The IRB form was submitted electronically and included: a general description of the proposed research, data collection tools, a description of the research participants, community research stakeholders and partners, potential risks and benefits, data confidentiality, potential conflicts of interest, informed consent, expedited review criteria, and final checklist and electronic signatures. The IRB approval number was 07-17-07-0142556.

Each participant was required to sign a consent form to become a part of the research. Participants could withdraw from the research at anytime via verbal request. Confidentially was ensured throughout the research process. Recorded data, transcription, notes, and other materials were to be stored and locked. After five years, the researcher will destroy all materials pertaining to participants.

Summary

A phenomenological research methodology was used to analyze motivation among African American women in leadership positions. A qualitative research design was selected for this research to study the natural phenomena of African American women through their experiences. The researcher used the interview as the chief instrument of the study.

The researcher's role included developing the Motivation Interview Protocol, functioning as the chief investigator, developing rapport with the National Black MBA Association as well as the participants, conducting the interviews, ensuring validity and respect for the participants, transcribing the data, analyzing the data, and summarizing the results. Chapter 4 illustrates the results of the telephone interviews, as well as the demographics of the participants.

CHAPTER 4: RESULTS AND FINDINGS

Introduction

The current study examined the experiences, motivation, barriers, and perceptions of 16 African American women in leadership positions in America corporations. The study utilized a qualitative research design with a phenomenological research method that examined the experiences and perceptions of motivation among the participants. The research was conducted via telephone interviews. The research problem was addressed by comparing the experiences of the participants with the motivational and leadership theories of thought leaders, as indicated in Chapter 2. To maintain continuity of the research, participants were asked the same 15 questions. Each interview question was designed to frame the answer to the research questions.

Research Questions

1. What factors do African American women perceive that motivate them to lead in American corporations?
2. What are some of the perceived barriers, if any, for African American women as they pursue leadership roles?

Methodology

This qualitative research was conducted to answer the question of what motivates African American women to lead in American corporations. A phenomenological approach was utilized to identify the experiences, barriers, and perceptions shared among the participants. The sample consisted of African American women currently in leadership positions. The data collection method was telephone interviews, and the analysis was based upon Moustakas (1994) research methods.

Sample

The research participants consisted of members of the National Black MBA Association, and participants obtained via snowballing. After obtaining IRB approval, the researcher made contact with potential participants. She used purposive sampling to identify potential African American female executives who were members of the National Black MBA Association. Ten of the 16 participants interviewed were members of the National Black MBA association, three were obtained via referrals (i.e., via snowballing) made by Sheryl Davis, the researcher's mentor, and the researcher referred three. As noted in Table 1, the participants' titles included CEO/president ($n = 1$), vice president ($n = 1$), senior accountant ($n = 1$), director ($n = 8$), manager ($n = 4$), and administrator ($n = 1$). Participants were 32 – 65 years old, with salaries from \$65,000 to more than \$130,000. All participants were of African American descent; one participant was bi-racial. Participants had held their jobs from nine months to 16 years. Participants resided within the United States, primarily in the Midwest, South, and East. All of the research participants were leaders within their respective corporations. Of the 16 participants interviewed, 11 had masters' degrees (two were pursuing a Ph.D.), one had a J.D., one had a Ph.D., two had bachelors' degrees, and one had a high school diploma. Each of the participants had experienced the phenomenon of being a leader in an American corporation. Two of the participants were dual career women, with the second career being entrepreneurial.

The researcher made initial contact to the Chicago Chapter of the National Black MBA association. However, the initial email contact was unsuccessful, because of no response from the Chicago Chapter. The researcher then contacted the headquarters of the National Black MBA Association. She contacted Lester McNair, member specialist of the National Black MBA Association, via telephone and email,. The researcher emailed the Participant's Letter Invitation (Appendix A), the Motivation Interview Protocol Appendix B), and Introduction Letter (Appendix C) to Mr. McNair to obtain approval of cooperation.

A follow-up email was sent to Mr. McNair to check the letter of cooperation (Appendix D) status. Upon Mr. McNair's approval, the letter was approved by Fred Phillips, III, director, Chapter Relations & Memberships Service (Appendix E). The letter of cooperation was dated and signed June 27, 2007. Both the National Black MBA Association and the researcher stipulated in writing, that the collected data would remain confidential regarding members' names, locations, and places of employment. Exceptions were the research committee and Walden University's IRB.

The researcher sent an e-blast (Appendix F) to the membership of the National Black MBA Association on July 20, 2007. The e-blast contained a synopsis of the research, as well as the researcher's email address and cellular telephone number.

Table 1. Participants' Demographics

Participant	Age	Salary	Years in Current Role	Position Title	Education
A	32	100K+	2	District Manager	MBA
B	29	65K	1	Senior Accountant	MBA
C	65	65-70K	16+	Administrator	MS
D	44	100-125K	4	Manager	MBA
E	36	105K	7	Director	MBA
F	36	1005+	3	Vice President	JD
G	41	85K	7	Director	MBA
H	35	90K	2	Chief Brand Strategist	MBA
I	57	132K	<1	Senior Director	HSD
J	43	60-80K	8	Project Manager/CEO	BS
K	56	150K	10	President	16+
L	40	100K	5	Project Manager/Entrepreneur	Master's
M	38	155K+	15	Director	Ph.D.
N	36	65K	0.8	Director	MBA
O	34	90-95K	25	Program Director	Dual Master's
P	43	100K+	0.9	Director	BS

Note: Race was deleted from the table since all participants were of African American descent; salary is reported in thousands of dollars (K); (MBA = Master of Business Administration; MS = Master of Science; HSD = High School Diploma; JD = Juris Doctorate; Ph.D. = Doctor of Philosophy; BS = Bachelor of Science)

Data Collection

The initial plan was to conduct face-to-face interviews with 15 participants. However, due to participants' locations,, time constraints, and work schedules, telephone interviews were obtained for 15, and one face-to-face interview was conducted. Sixteen interviews were conducted because initial contact was made with Participant P before ending the research. However, once 15 participants were obtained, the researcher decided to increase the sample size to include Participant P.

The researcher conducted the interviews, with an average time of 30 – 45 minutes, during July and August of 2007. Each interview was recorded on separate cassettes labeled with the participant's letter and date of the interview (e.g., Participant A-6-12-07). Participants associated with the National Black MBA Association responded to the e-blast via email within seven days. Once a potential participant emailed the researcher to express interest in the research, a follow-up email (Appendix G) was sent to the participant, which included the Participant's Invitation letter and the Motivation Protocol Interview, for review prior to the interview date. During the initial email, participants were asked to reply with a potential interview date and time.

Of the 17 members of the National Black MBA Association who responded, 10 were interviewed for the research. A follow-up email (Appendix H) was sent August 7 to Mr. McNair stating that six members of the National Black MBA Association were interviewed. Mr. McNair sent the e-blast to chapter presidents of the National Black MBA Association, Inc. requesting participation. The additional four participants were chapter presidents of the National Black MBA Association.

Six participants who were not members of the National Black MBA Association received a telephone call from the researcher, inviting them to participate in the research, followed by an email (Appendix I), which included the Participation Invitation and the Motivation Protocol Interview. With the exception of the initial telephone call, both groups of participants went through the same introduction and pre-interview process.

Before recording the interview, the researcher described the purpose of the research and instructed the participant to say "not applicable" to questions the participant was uncomfortable answering. The research reiterated to the participant that the participant's name and place of employment would be confidential. Two of the participants who also were entrepreneurs requested that the researcher list their businesses in the dissertation. The researcher instructed them to state the name of the organization during the interview. The interview also asked each participant if she had any questions before recording the interview. During the interview, the Motivation Interview Protocol was read, indicating the title of the dissertation, time, date, place, interview, and interviewee, and was labeled with the corresponding letter of the alphabet. After the interview, the participants were notified when the recording was stopped. The researcher asked each participant if she had any additional questions. The participants also were notified that they would receive a transcript, via email, within 48 to 72 hours after the interview. The participants were encouraged, verbally and via email, (Appendix J) to make any corrections to the transcript to ensure its accuracy. After the member check was completed, the researcher used the edited transcript as the data for the research (Appendix K). Ten of the 16 participants interviewed successfully completed the member check process by editing the original transcript.

During the interviewing process, notes were made only to code participants' identities and during the demographic section of the interview, which aided in creating the transcripts. The transcripts initially were created verbatim; then adjustments were made to exclude unnecessary jargon (such as *umms* and creative thoughts between sentences). To enhance the reliability and validity of the transcript, and ensure verification, the researcher requested that participants conduct a member check.

In addition, participants were encouraged to submit an electronically signed copy of their invitation, which was the consent to the interview. Several of the participants did not want their names revealed in any aspect of the research; therefore, the email indicating the date and time of the interview was used to indicate the consent to interview. The participants' consents, recorded data, and transcripts will be stored and locked for five years. After five years, the researcher will destroy all material pertaining to the research.

Research Questions Results and Findings

Research Question 1: What factors do African American women perceive to motivate them to lead in American corporations?

Three questions on the interview addressed motivation. The first question was framed to identify what motivated the participants to pursue a leadership role, the second question asked the participants to define motivation, and the third question asked the participants to identify their top five motivators. The participants' responses to what motivated them to pursue a leadership role was scattered: seven participants referenced their family (in particular, their parents) or the community, and five referenced an internal desire to lead as a motivator in a leadership role.

Of the 16 participants interviewed, 13 defined motivation as something that is internal. Three participants defined motivation as influencing others. The question that asked the participants to identify their top five motivators was placed at the end of the Motivation Interview Protocol to provide the participants the opportunity to build upon their responses to previous questions. The answer to the research question of what motivates African American women to lead in American corporations was divided into seven areas. Twelve of the 16 participants listed family as one of their five motivators, eight participants listed the desire to succeed, eight listed the community/people, seven listed faith, seven listed money, six listed recognition, and five listed personal growth/

development. Participant F did not answer Question Number 14. Table 2 provides a synopsis of the top seven motivators, in order of priority, as identified by the participants. The corresponding number of times the participants provided each response is adjacent to the motivator.

Table 2. Participants' Motivators

Motivator	Times Referenced
Family	12
Desire to succeed	8
Community/People	8
Money	7
Faith	7
Recognition	6
Personal growth/Development	5

Research Question 2: What are some of the perceived barriers, if any, for African American women as they pursue leadership roles?

Two prompts addressed research question number two. Participant G stated that one of her barriers was "the lack of savvy from a political perspective, knowing how to maneuver your way through the process." All 16 participants made statements that related to the above statement, which included the lack of networks, the lack of mentors, and the lack of knowledge of the corporation's politics. Eleven of the participants noted discrimination (for example, based on race, gender, or age) as a barrier to pursuing leadership roles. Perceived notions about African American women, such as the belief that African American woman are "angry black women" was stated to be a barrier among seven of the African American women interviewed. Seven indicated that overcoming the belief of perceived notions, as well as maintaining their composure during adversity to denounce the belief also were challenges.

Interview Question Results and Findings

Moustakas's (1994) modification of van Kaam's (1966) method of analysis was utilized to analyze the data of the research. The process consisted of horizonalization, clustering and thematizing the invariant constituents, and establishing a composite textural-structural description of the research based upon the research questions. For the horizonalization process, the researcher listed the questions, followed by each participant's response to the question, to identify a cluster of meanings and themes. A sample of the horizonalization process is provided in the next section.

Horizonalization

Question 1: What motivated you to pursue a leadership role?

Participant A

> Gosh, I guess part of it was just to have challenging work and a different responsibility; and then probably from a motivation standpoint; just drive would be money as a motivator, status as a motivator, and probably my parents as being my strongest support system, wanting to please them as well.

Participant B

> A lot of factors influenced my decision in wanting to attain leadership roles in my career. First, would definitely be my mother. She was and still is an educator, and she instilled in my siblings and me not to settle for less. Why work for a company, when you could own your own company and lead it…she'd ask. Secondly, my experiences in corporate America helped gauge me in wanting to lead an organization. Lastly, overall, my skill set has equipped me in being able to be an effective leader,

hone my organizational skills and communication skills, which are vital to any organization.

Participant C

Well, I have always been involved in politics, community organizations, and things of that nature, which I got from my mom. I saw so many children in the neighborhood who needed help and guidance. I was actively involved in the Girl Scouts. I was a teen adviser for younger children. I was seen as a leader within the community at a very young age. When I started working for Congressman Danny Davis, I really became involved with the children within the community. I saw so many things that I could do within the community to help motivate children. So I went to college and received my degree in juvenile justice. I continue to work for Mr. Davis. I really was not active with what I really wanted to do, which was working with young adults. So I joined the staff as an administrator.

Participant D

I was encouraged to pursue this role because of the opportunity. As leader of an affinity group, I get to not only to help the organization, but also to help other African Americans here working at my company.

Participant E

I was actually promoted into a leadership role, so I did not necessarily pursue it.

Participant F

I guess it goes back to when I was a small child, probably, my mother encouraged me. I have been involved since I was a little kid in a lot of activities, dating all the way back, I ran for the Homecoming Queen of the Pee Wee Football Team. My mom started me on that path. I got involved in politics when I was really young. My mom would take me around political campaigns. I saw my mom working on the board of directors of different agencies and volunteering, she was always a leader in our small town. She gave me the courage to go out and try things that no one else had really tried. Going back to 10th grade, I was treasurer of my class, junior class VP, and senior class president. I was active in college, president of my sorority; I went on to become the first African American president of my student body, at my law school. It just counterplots from there. As far back as I can remember I was in some sort of leadership position.

Participant G

I had a strong educational foundation, and coming from a large family there were many leadership opportunities around the breakfast or dinner table. So, my parents were very bent on education as a way of propelling you, or putting you in a leadership position, or in the forefront or whatever. That started by having open discussions around the table, sharing our opinion. As well as my personal continuous quest to do better, and become better, self-actualization, if you will. I think I had a strong cultural of leadership around me growing up.

Participant H

Leadership has always motivated me. It was instilled in me as a child through school, being a leader in different activities that I had a lot of passion for, or that I was good at, different clubs, and other extra curricular activities. In college, it was the same thing. So, when I graduated and started my first job in Cambridge, MA,

I was really driven by wanting to: (1) perform well, (2) be recognized as a valuable asset to the community (by both my management team as well as my peers), and (3) to really take ownership of the work that I did, and to do it with the best of my ability.

Participant I

It was not my dream; it was not what I started out to do. I was at a company and I was considered a business analyst, and the only way to advance past a certain level was to enter into a leadership role.

Participant J

I think it is in my genes, being the oldest in my family; I got my genes from my father. I have always been in organizations where I have been in a leadership position.

Participant K

I think I have primarily been motivated by, (1) my family, my rearing, and upbringing, (2) by the kinds of role models and mentors with whom I interacted as I moved through the educational system, and beyond to my corporate life. I think the lives of the women and of course, my mother and father who always encouraged me to always strive for success motivated me to pursue a leadership role. They taught me lessons that would suggest that good enough never is…it always was a driver for me. No matter how impoverished my family was, and by the way, I didn't even know I was poor until I got to high school; where I didn't wear a different dress everyday for two weeks as some of my friend did. It was a really rich opportunity for me to learn by looking at positive examples.

Participant L

> I was motivated to take on a leadership role to be a role model to a lot African Americans within the community, and to let them know that there are pathways in which that can actually follow to see people of their own color, people who have taken on education beyond some of the limitations that past generations have faced. I just wanted to take that to another level and progress for our community, and for our people.

Participant M

> I would say…I don't know if anything motivated me to pursue a leadership role. I think it was just something that was more over a period of my career that I was always pressed into leadership positions. It was something that just kind of happened over a period of time. I don't think I was driven or motivated to seek, or pursue a leadership role. I just kind of walked into the kind of work that I like to do.

Participant N

> I guess it was just the expectation of being a leader and the experiences and opportunities that come along with that. You are seen in a different light, and often times, more opportunities present themselves when you are in a leadership role. It is about opportunities.

Participant O

> I have always known that I wanted to be in health care. I have always had concerns in regards to health care and minorities, as it relates to access to, whether lack of access to health care. I knew that if I ever wanted to be in a position to initiate change, then I would have

to be in a position of upper management in order to initiate change and implement some of the programs that I wanted to do. By the virtue of my final outcome, a leadership position was the only way I would ever make it happen.

Participant P

I am a person who believes that motivation is something that is internal. So that being said, the word motivation derived from the word motive. A motive comes from the inside. I actually didn't pursue a leadership role. It was in me, I believe, as a child to be a leader. I have never known how not to be a leader. I just happened to find a position that suited that leadership ability that I already had, and that is not a pompous statement. It is just a reality. I have always been motivated to pursue the next level, whatever that next level maybe. Whether it is in business, my personal life, or my fun time, I am always pursuing the next level. I am naturally motivated to lead.

Cluster of Meaning and Thematizing

The second phase of Moustakas's analysis includes reducing and eliminating to establish the invariant constituents. Each answer was reviewed to evaluate its relevance and significance to the research. Horizons were identified based upon their significance to the understanding of the research, as well as their ability to abstract and to label the experience (Moustakas, 1994). Statements that did not meet the above criteria were removed during the elimination phase.

The third phase of Moustakas's (1994) analysis is clustering and thematizing the invariant constituents of the African American women leaders. A list of themes was developed based upon the answers transcribed during the interview process. Below is a list of the seven themes:

1. *Motivation is intrinsic.*

The data indicated that most participants defined motivation as internal, an internal force or influence, or something that comes from within. Participants identified family ($n = 12$), community/people ($n = 8$), the desire to succeed ($n = 8$), money ($n = 7$), spirituality/faith ($n = 7$), recognition ($n = 6$), and personal growth/development ($n = 5$) as top motivators. As noted by the above list, many participants listed intrinsic factors as motivators. The extrinsic factors listed were family, community/people, and money.

The following were some of their responses:

   a. "My personal continuous quest to do better, and become better, self actualization, if you will. Motivation is a personal thing…my spirituality. I am grounded spiritually and emotionally" (Participant G).

   b. "Leadership has always motivated me. I would define motivation as the drive one has to fulfill a dream, or passion, or a need without encouragement, or expression by others… my faith" (Participant H).

   c. "I think it is in my genes… I am motivated by God, my father" (Participant J).

   d. "I am motivated by (1) self fulfillment, (2) the drive to be recognize as extremely savvy, competent, and confident, (3) acknowledgement by people who I care about acknowledging my ability or my success by those that I respect" (Participant K).

   e. "My top five motivators are (1) spiritual; I am spiritually motivated to do things in my might in a Godly fashion" (Participant L).

2. *Ignorance is a barrier.*

The lack of knowledge of the cultural beliefs, ethics, character, and behavior of African Americans, according to the participants, continues to be a barrier, and challenge as it relates to growth and promotions. Another challenge expressed by participants was the lack of corporate knowledge and awareness among African Americans.

The following statements were captured during the interviewing processes:

    a. "Sometimes the challenges that I feel I faced are ones that were already there years and years before, that I am trying to break the barriers and establish myself as well as my female colleagues, or more importantly my African American counterparts" (Participant B).

    b. "Working through the reams of mess! The disrespect, even though it is subtle disrespect. The differences that are made between African Americans and Caucasians in the recognition you receive for your achievements" (Participant I)

    c. "Being underestimated, definitely, which sometimes is amusing, because you do not have to flaunt your intelligence or your experience, your performance will speak for itself" (Participant E).

    d. "Therefore that means that sometimes I must control my tone and I must control my temper" (Participant F).

    e. "My greatest challenge is overcoming preconceived notions that my team members have about the way that I should lead or the way that I should be" (Participant H).

3. *Leadership is situational.*

The data suggested that participants tailor their leadership style to the needs and expectations of employees, with the emphasis on achieving corporate goals. Twelve of the participants indicated that they include employees in their leadership decisions. Some of the excerpts are as follows:

a. "I lead by needs. I identify the needs of my employees and students and coach them by their specific needs and or situation" (Participant C).

b. "I would say it depends on the person I am interacting with…My most natural and comfortable style is probably consultative leadership" (Participant A).

c. "I tend to try to maximize the talent and skill of the individual so it is individual driven. If the individual is very talented and skilled, I probably have a more hands off approach, and just provide coaching and guiding, as needed" (Participant E).

d. "I like to think it is transformational, but in my experiences, I know I have to apply various styles as the situation warrants. Sometimes I have to be decisive, sometimes I have to be more transactional because you have to deal with the situation at that time, but overall, I want to be a leader who listens and involves people" (Participant G).

e. "Right now, my leadership style is more inclusive. I like to include the group" (Participant J).

4. *Leaders should lead by example and serve.*

Each participant studied defined leadership as being an example, being a servant, providing service, influencing, or inspiring people. Five of the participants referenced the word "example" in their reply. Listed below are some of the statements captured during the interview process:

a. "Leadership for me is servant-ship. I have learned that in my life, in my religious life, in my personal life that the greatest leaders are those who are willing to serve" (Participant P).

b. "The true definition of leadership to me is someone who not only talks the talk, but also walks the walk. I think that a true leader is someone who is a visionary, and knows how to inspire others on their team to move in the direction of that vision" (Participant O).

c. "I guess it is more so leading in a way in which inspires other people to want to lead" (Participant N).

d. "Leadership is the ability to galvanize and engage people, in such a way as, to convince them without convincing them that they need to work toward a certain end" (Participant K).

e. "I would say that leadership is leading by example. Leadership is being an example. My philosophy would be lead by example" (Participant J).

5. *Discrimination is a driving force.*

When participants were questioned about the impact of discrimination on their careers, 10 said it was a propelling motivator or it had a positive impact during their career. Some of the statements reflecting this theme included:

a. "It has had a heavy impact on my career; but again, I believe that it fuels my success" (Participant B).

b. "I definitely dealt with discrimination at all levels of my career. I guess it made me a more determined individual" (Participant E).

c. "I know I have had to work twice as hard as the next person does. This is why I have had to keep my nose clean and stay out of trouble and do what I was supposed to be doing" (Participant F).

d. "Discrimination has been something that I have experienced on certainly more than one occasion. If anything, it has made me firmer in my resolve to achieve at the highest levels of whatever I chose to undertake, rather it was a senior level position in corporate America" (Participant K).

Motivating Change

    e. "Discrimination actually drives me to go faster. It drives me to want to go beyond any limitations" (Participant L).

6. *Mentorship is needed and impactful.*

The data suggested that African American women believe mentorship is needed and is impactful in obtaining a leadership position. Eleven of the 16 African American leaders interviewed had some form of mentor during their career. Listed below is a sample of the responses to questions about mentorship:

    a. "I had mentors and they had a very positive impact on my career, as well as my future. Mentors are very valuable. We must ensure that our youth have mentors to help them through the process" (Participant C).

    b. "You need to have someone kind of share how they overcame a particular barrier" (Participant D).

    c. "Mentorship means everything, it is exposure and opportunity…" (Participant F).

    d. "As a professional, I have not had a lot of mentoring, that is one of the things I feel would have helped me to be a stronger leader or in a stronger position" (Participant G).

    e. "Wow, it was huge. It had a huge impact" (Participant H).

7. *Maintain a winning attitude.*

When asked to provide advice to future generations, each participant offered information that related to being successful, reaching for dreams, and being positive. Below are some excerpts from the interviews:

    a. "If you work smarter and not harder it really means just being efficient, being organized, and planning, you can achieve the career goals, as well as the family, and having a personal life, and all of that as well" (Participant A).

b. "You can be anybody and anything that you want to be, if you make the decision to do it" (Participant F).

c. "Whatever you decide to do, whatever you put your mind to do, be the best you can be, and give it every effort, and look at every avenue without giving up. Do not allow anything to be a deterrent for you" (Participant G).

d. "Be positive and proactive about enhancing those things they want to enhance about themselves" (Participant H).

e. "You think the whole world is out there against you, and it is not. It is just there waiting for you; all you have to do is go and get it" (Participant O).

Composite Textural-structural Description

The data suggested that African American women are motivated by intrinsic and extrinsic factors. The intrinsic factors indicated as motivators were the desire to succeed, faith, recognition, and personal growth/development. The extrinsic factors indicated as motivators were family, community/people, and money. The experiences of the participants were clustered into seven themes, including: motivation is intrinsic, ignorance is a barrier, discrimination is a driving force, mentorship is needed and impactful, leadership is situational, leaders should lead by example and serve, and maintaining a winning attitude.

Triangulation

The researcher examined seven motivation theories as a form of quality of standard verification to interpret the research. This procedure, or triangulation, was used to answer the question of what is motivation to African American female leaders. The process included corroborating the evidence from the process, needs, and reinforcement theories, and exploring the perspectives of the participants. Triangulation interpretation suggested that the African American female leaders in the current study define motivation as intrinsic, and that their experiences resembled the beliefs of the needs theorists.

Gagne (2005) believed that humans who are motivated by intrinsic factors seek to find satisfaction and interest within an activity. This means that humans perform different work related tasks simply because they enjoy performing the tasks. Intrinsic motivation is a behavior reinforced by learned behavior (Maslow, 1987). This learned behavior is reinforced by pleasure and enjoyment obtained in completing the task or performing the job successfully. All of the participants studied defined motivation as an internal force, which directly relates to the belief that humans are motivated by intrinsic factors. The intrinsic factors that were perceived to motivate the participants studied also provides similarity to the needs theory of Maslow (1987), Herzberg (1997), McClelland and Winter (1969), and Alderfer (Miner, 2002).

The Encyclopedia Britannica (n.d.) identified a need as an aspect of life that is essential to survive. A basic need may be characterized by some as food, water, nutrition, or safety. Other people may view needs as shelter, love, belonging, and peace of mind. Although needs are labeled as essential to life, the humanistic theorists, such as Maslow (1987), believed that motivation is based upon unmet needs that are met through levels of hierarchies. McClelland believed that achievement, authority, and affiliation motivate humans to achieve objectives. Herzberg's theory is based upon two components: hygiene factors and motivators. Both must be done simultaneously to achieve desired outcomes within the work environment. These needs are far more inclusive than the traditional basic needs such as food and water. This statement means achievement of motivational factors that are intangible requires energy from intrinsic motivation. Although each theorist provides a different theory of needs, each lists a common theme centered upon the importance of satisfying a need as a means of motivation within human behavior. This desire to satisfy unmet needs is believed to be the motivational factor in human behavior and development, according to Maslow (1987).

Summary

Chapter 4 provided an analysis of the data, including demographic profiles of the participants interviewed. The research questions and purpose of the research was reiterated, as well as findings associated with the results. Moustakas' method of analysis was used to analyze the finding of the 15 interview questions. Seven themes emerged from the in-depth interviews, which included: motivation is intrinsic, ignorance is a barrier, discrimination is a driving force, mentorship is needed and impactful, leadership is situational, leaders should lead by example and serve, and maintain a winning attitude. The discussion, conclusion, recommendations for further studies, and implications for social change are presented in Chapter 5.

CHAPTER 5: SUMMARY, CONCLUSION, AND RECOMMENDATIONS

Summary, Conclusion, and Recommendations

The purpose of this phenomenological research was to understand what motivated 16 African American women to lead in American corporations. The research was conducted via purposive sampling with the cooperation of the National Black MBA Association. In-depth telephone interviews from 30 to 45 minutes were recorded and transcribed to document the experiences of the female leaders. Moustakas' method of analysis, which included horizonalization, clustering of meaning, and texture description, was used to analyze the findings of the interviews.

The following research questions were explored:
1. What factors do African American women perceive to motivate them to lead in American corporations?
2. What are some of the perceived barriers, if any, for African American women as they pursue leadership roles?

The results suggested that the African American women studied were motivated by the following intrinsic factors and extrinsic factors: family, community/people, money, faith, the desire to succeed, recognition, and personal growth/development. The perceived barriers noted by the African American leaders were: discrimination; perceived notions of the work ethic, behavior, and academic abilities of African Americans; the lack of knowledge of internal politics; lack of mentorship; and lack of networking outlets.

Conceptual/Theoretical Framework

The phenomenological research explored the experience of 16 African American women. Fifteen open-ended questions were asked using in-depth interview as the data collection method. The research aimed to determine what motivates African American women in leadership positions to become leaders within American corporations. Data collected during telephone interviews provided the basis for general and universal meanings of motivation and the barriers experienced by these women, and was linked to existing motivation theories in the literature. Common bonds and patterns were identified and conceptualized into themes and a composite narrative description of the participants' shared experiences via a procedure called meaning structuring through narratives (Kvale, 1996).

The findings suggested that African American women are motivated by intrinsic factors that are related to the needs theory of Maslow (1987), McClelland and Winter (1969), Herzberg (1997), and Alderfer (Miner, 2002). The experiences shared by the participants were similar to the needs theories analyzed in chapter 2 of the research. The results of this phenomenological research also suggested that African American women display a combination of the servant leader (Greenleaf, 2002), the positional leader (Maxwell, 2000), and the situational leader (Blanchard et al., 1985). The participants believed that leaders should lead by example as well as lead according to particular situations.

Implications for Social Change

The problem addressed in this study was the lack of academic research on what motivates African American women to lead in American corporations. With the publication of this study, the social change impact is an awareness and understanding of the intrinsic and extrinsic motivation factors of African American women in leadership roles, in the form of an academic research. The development of understanding and awareness of the barriers and motivating factors of African American women in leadership positions will assist in the ability to cause change in the mindset of corporations, the community, and organizations. With the knowledge that motivation is intrinsic for African American women, with the predominate motivator coming from the family, corporations and organizations are encouraged to focus on promoting work-life balance for employees. Because of this study, corporations also have the data supporting the work ethic, drive, character, behavior, and ambition of African American women, and to denounce perceived notions within the workplace that are incorrect. It provides a call for action to all corporations to provide information regarding the diversity of the customer, which should include diversity education for employees and leaders on the history and culture of not only African Americans but also all minority groups.

Based on the results of this study, the researcher provided recommendations to the National Black MBA Association Inc. to encourage the incorporation of mentorship programs and network building initiatives among its members to enhance development and growth and to encourage more African Americans within the executive boards of American corporations. Another social implication is implied for the next generation of African American leaders, which is to obtain a winning attitude, to pursue education, and to exceed all expectations. An abstract of the research was disseminated to each participant and to the National Black MBA Association via email.

Recommendations for Further Study

The recommendation for further study is needed for women in general. Although this study was about African American women specifically, further studies should be conducted to identify any differences in the motivating factors of men and women and to explore how motivation affects the ability for each group to become leaders

within an organization. Further studies also are needed to answer the following questions:
1. How do family members motivate African Americans to lead?
2. What impact does the family have on the motivation of African American men?
3. What impact does mentorship have on the African American community?

Conclusion

For African American females, barriers of discrimination and stereotyping continue to be present within American corporations. The quest to understand what motivated 16 African American women leaders to pursue a leadership role in American corporations spanned beyond extrinsic factors. Intrinsic factors such as the desire to succeed, faith, recognition, and personal growth/development propelled many African American women into leadership positions. Participants also listed extrinsic factors such as: money, family, and community/people as motivators. Academic documentation of motivation pertaining to African American women has the ability to educate organizations, corporations, networks, and community groups in developing programs, such as mentorship partnerships, to increase the amount of African American female leaders within American corporations.

REFERENCES

Adams, J. S. (1963). *Inequity in social exchange. Advances in experimental social psychology.* New York: Academic Press.

Bass, B., & Stogdill, R. (1990). *Bass & Stogdill's handbook of leadership.* New York: The Free Press.

Baumeister, R., & Leary, M. (1995). The need to belong: Desire for interpersonal attachments as a fundamental human motivation. *Psychological Bulletin, 117,* 497-529.

Bennis, W. (2000). *Managing the dream reflections on leadership and change.* Cambridge: Perseus Publishing.

Blake, R., & Mouton, J. (1985). *The managerial grid III.* Houston, TX: Gulf Publishing Company, Book Division.

Blanchard, K., & Johnson, S. (2003). *The one minute manager.* New York: HarperCollins book

Blanchard, K., Zigarmi, P., & Zigarmi, D. (1985). *Leadership and the one minute manager.* New York: William Morrow and Company, Inc.

Burns, J. (2003). *Transforming leadership.* New York: Atlantic Monthly Press.

Burns, J. (1978). *Leadership.* New York: Harper and Row Publishers.

Catalyst Report. (2002). *Catalyst census of women corporate officers and top earners.* Retrieved April 30, 2007, from http://www.catalyst.org/ knowledge/titles/ title.php?page=cen_COTE_06

Catalyst Report. (2003). *Catalyst women in US corporate leadership.* Retrieved April 30, 2007, from http://www.catalyst.org/ knowledge/titles /title.php?page =lead_ wuscl_03

Catalyst Report. (2007). *Damned or doomed. Catalyst study on gender stereotyping at work uncovers double-blind dilemmas for women.* Retrieved August 11, 2007 from http://www.catalystwomen.org/pressroom/pressdoublebind.shtml

Cobbs, P., & Turnock, J. (2003). *Cracking the corporate code.* New York: Amacom.

Creswell, J. (1998). *Qualitative inquiry and research design choosing among five traditions.* London: Sage Publications.

Daniels, C. (2004). *Black Power, Inc.* Hoboken, NJ: John Wiley & Sons, Inc.

Dunn, L. (2002). Theories of learning. *Oxford Centre for Staff and Learning Development, 1,* 1-3.

Encyclopedia Britannica (n.d). Retrieved August 21, 2005, from http://www.britannica.com/search?query=motivation&ct=&searchSubmit.x=14&searchSubmit.y=12

Franklin, J., & Meier, A. (Eds.). (1982). *Black leaders of the twentieth century.* Chicago: University of Illinois Press.

Gagne, M. (2005). Self-determination theory and work motivation. *Journal of Organization Behavior, 26,* 331-362.

Goenwald, T. (2004). Phenomenological research design. *International Journal of Qualitative Methods, 3,* 1.

Greenleaf, R. (2002). *Servant leadership.* Mahwah, NJ: Paulist Press.

Hammond, M., Howarth, J., & Keat, R. (1991), *Understanding phenomenology*. Cambridge, MA: Basil Blackwell.

Herzberg, F. (1997). *The Motivation to work*. Piscataway, New Jersey: Transaction Publishers.

Halepota, H. (2005). Motivational theories and their application in construction. *Cost Engineering, 47*, 14-18.

Kvale, S. (1996). *Interview: An introduction to qualitative research interviewing*. London: Sage Publications.

Marshall, C., & Rossman, G. (1995). *Designing qualitative research* (2nd Ed.). London: Sage Publications.

Maxwell, J. (1993). *Developing the leader within you*. Nashville, TN: Thomas Nelson, Inc.

Maxwell, J. (2000). *The 21 most powerful minutes in a leader's day*. Nashville, TN: Thomas Nelson, Inc.

Maslow, A. H. (1987). *Motivation and Personality* (3rd Ed.). New York: Longman.

McClelland, D., & Winter, D. (1969). *Motivating economic achievement*. New York: The Free Press.

Miner, J. (2002). *Organizational behavior: Foundations, theories, and analyses*. New York: Oxford University Press.

Moustakas, C. (1994). *Phenomenology research methods*. Thousand Oaks, CA: Sage.

National Center for Education Statistics. (2002). *U. S. Department of Education, Digest of Education Statistics.* Retrieved April 27, 2007, from http://nces.ed.gov/

Nierenberg, S., & Fong, S. (2006). Rate of women's advancement to top corporate officer positions slow, new Catalyst tenth anniversary census reveals. Retrieved April 30, 2007, from http://www.catalyst.org/pressroom/releases_06.shtml

Parker, P. (2005). *Race, gender, and leadership.* Mahwah, NJ: Lawrence Erlbaum Associates, Publishers.

Singleton, R., & Straits, B. (2005). *Approaches to social research* (4th Ed.). New York: Oxford University Press.

Skinner, B. (1953). *Science and human behavior.* New York: The Free Press.

Thorndike, E. (1932). *The fundamentals of learning.* New York: Teachers College Press.

van Kaam, A. (1966). *Application of the phenomenological method.* Lanham, MD: University Press of America.

Vroom, V. H. (1995). *Work and motivation.* San Francisco: Jossey-Bass.